THE BRITISH MUSEUM

VISITOR'S GUIDE
WORLD RELIGIONS

Self-guided tours

John Reeve

Thanks and Acknowledgements

*Thanks to Carla Turchini for design; Coralie Hepburn,
Nina Shandloff and Beatriz Waters at the British
Museum Press; the British Museum Department of
Photography and Imaging; and everyone who read
and commented or advised on the text.*
JFR

above
Hindu shrine (see p.50).

opposite
The god Shiva (see p.50).

previous page
The Angel Gabriel (see pp.70-1).

Front cover illustrations (*top to bottom*): details of statue of the
Buddha; icon of John the Baptist; painting of Shiva; Islamic glass.

© 2006 The Trustees of the British Museum

John Reeve has asserted the right to be identified as
the author of this work

First published in 2006 by The British Museum Press
A division of The British Museum Company Ltd
38 Russell Square, London WC1B 3QQ
www.britishmuseum.org

Reprinted 2007, 2008

ISBN 978-0-7141-5040-6

A catalogue record for this book is available from
the British Library

Photography by the British Museum Department
of Photography and Imaging
Tour maps adapted by Turchini Design Ltd
Designed and typeset in Bliss by Turchini Design Ltd
Printed and bound in Italy by Printer Trento

Mixed Sources
Product group from well-managed
forests and other controlled sources
www.fsc.org Cert no. CQ-COC-000012
© 1996 Forest Stewardship Council
FSC

Contents

How to use this guide

There is no right way to visit the British Museum – it's up to you, and how much time and energy you have.

If this is your first visit you might want to take Tour 2 as an introductory tour. You could also use the **British Museum Visitor's Guide** (same format as this Guide) and take the introductory first tour. Or you could take a live tour (see opposite).

If you find walking tiring you might prefer to concentrate on the tours which focus on only one or two galleries (Tours 4, 5, 6).

You can return to the Great Court at any time for information, tours, tickets, shops or for coffee, lunch or tea.

To find out more about the objects you see or the cultures from which they come, use the **Paul Hamlyn Library** (off **2**). The Museum's digital database is also available there, as well as online at *www.britishmuseum.org/research*.

Note that numbers in bold refer to gallery numbers.
Case numbers are usually in the top left-hand corner of cases.

NOTE ON DATES: The British Museum uses standard BC/AD dates in all its labels and publications, a style also followed here. The Islamic calendar uses AH (meaning after the Hijra, the emigration of Muhammad from Mecca to Medina in AD 622), so the year 1 AH is roughly equivalent to AD 622.

The dome of the restored round Reading Room (1854–7), in which Karl Marx wrote *Das Kapital*.

Other tours of the Museum

Highlights tours by professional tourist guides will introduce you to some of the major cultures. Enquire and book at the Great Court Audio Tour Desk.

EyeOpener tours by specially trained volunteer guides introduce individual galleries or specific areas of the collection, 10 times or more a day. Meet in the gallery: details in a special leaflet and in 'What's on', available free from the Information Desk and Box Office.

Gallery talks by curators and educators, along with many other special events such as lectures, study days, courses, films, performances and family activities, are also listed in 'What's on'.

Audio tours (available from the Great Court Audio Tour Desk):

Highlights audio tour
Short commentaries on some of the most important star objects and less well-known artefacts from the Museum's collection. Available in English, Spanish and Japanese.

Family audio tour
Join Stephen Fry on a trail of bodies, beasts and board games.

Enlightenment Gallery audio tour
Neil MacGregor, Director of the British Museum, is your guide to the permanent exhibition called Enlightenment: Discovering the World in the 18th Century (**1**), displayed in the magnificently restored room formerly known as the King's Library.

Parthenon audio tour
In-depth commentaries on the Parthenon sculptures by curator Ian Jenkins. Available in seven languages from the Parthenon galleries (**18**).

For further information see pp. 92–4 for more sources, including links to other relevant museums and websites.

Introduction

THERE IS NO DISTINCTION BETWEEN RELIGION AND THE REST OF LIFE ... ALL OF LIFE IS RELIGIOUS.

African saying

THAT WHICH IS ONE, THE WISE CALL BY MANY NAMES.

Rig Veda (early Hindu text), c.900 BC

Museums offer us the opportunity to look at the religious art and cultures of many societies, past and present and – unusually – side by side. Of course, the examples of religious art that survive in museums can never comprehensively reflect any religious practice, nor can they cover a complete geographical and time range. Inevitably, much of what is on display is about death rather than life, showing an overriding concern, whether in ancient Egypt or modern Africa, with appropriate burial and rituals for the dead.

The British Museum is an especially rewarding place in which to consider what religion means and has meant across diverse cultures and centuries, and what meanings can be drawn from the evidence. These meanings will be personal to each visitor, but this guide book can help to point out where the evidence is, and to suggest some connections.

Every religion changes complexion as it moves into new settings and eras. Moving around the world and through time as we walk around the Museum hints at these changes. Re-examining ancient religions can shed light not only on the ancient cultures which practised them but also on living religions in our own times, although we must also guard against the potential for misunderstanding oral and prehistoric cultures when interpreted through modern eyes.

The 21st century is witnessing a growing interest in religion, and for a host of reasons: dissatisfaction with a global, consumerist world culture; the search for protective frameworks to support different identities and world-views; and a return to tradition when those world-views are attacked, misunderstood and misrepresented. New cathedrals, mosques and Hindu temples are being built today. Contemporary artists and composers continue to draw on religious inspiration, as did their predecessors: requiems are still being composed as well as other music inspired by Greek and Russian Orthodox and many other traditions.

Marble figurine of a woman, Cyclades, prehistoric Greece (c.2700–2500 BC). (**11**, *case 3*)

Virgin and Child, ivory, France (14th century). (**40**)

Making connections

Seeing religious art together helps to make connections and draw common themes. Animals, for example, are symbols of respect and fear in religions as different as native North American and ancient Egyptian. A giant scarab beetle pushed the sun across the sky for the ancient Egyptians, while for the ancient Greeks the sun and moon were both driven across the sky in chariots drawn by horses.

Mountains and rocks were sacred in ancient Greece and Japan, Australia, India and Mexico and also in the world of Moses. Different trees housed different gods for the ancient Greeks. Water was where ancient Greek and Celtic gods lived and where the Celts made offerings, while in Islam it is important for purification. Floods figure in the literature of Jews, Christians and Hindus, as well as the cultures of ancient Mesopotamia.

Sometimes one faith supplants another as the result of violent disruption and persecution. Zoroastrianism was replaced as the religion of Iran after 1000 years, surviving mainly among the Parsees in India and East Africa. Sometimes different faiths coexist fairly happily and play significant roles at different rites of passage within the same culture, as in Japan with Shintō, Christianity and Buddhism.

Sometimes there is continuity on one sacred site over many centuries, from one faith to another: Jerusalem and Mecca are obvious examples. Another is Cordoba in Spain, where after the expulsion of the Moors in 1492 the cathedral was built inside a mosque, which itself stood on the site of an earlier Roman temple and Visigothic church. In modern London, the building that currently houses Spitalfields mosque has been a chapel for French Huguenots and then Methodists, and later a Jewish synagogue, continually responding to the needs of new waves of immigrants and refugees.

Often an object's meaning is completely transformed as it changes hands and cultures. The Elizabethan magus Dr Dee used a mysterious Aztec obsidian disc for his magic; it was then acquired as a curiosity by an 18th-century collector and is now used to illustrate the mindset of the Enlightenment (**1**, *case 20*). In the next section we can see how a similar transformation in meaning occurred with a sculpture from Polynesia.

Tara, gilt bronze, Sri Lanka (7th–8th century). (**33**)

Reading religious art

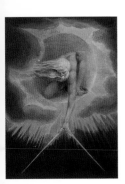

William Blake, 'God creating the Universe', etching (1794).

All faiths have ways of explaining and representing the creation of the world and of humans. In Hinduism, for instance, a golden egg floats on the primeval waters, and the god Shiva dances, balancing creation and destruction *(see p.3 and Tour 4)*.

Here are two other, very different views of creation from the 18th century, one English and the other Polynesian.

This poem about A'a (also known as Ta'aroa) comes from Hawaii:

> *He existed, Ta'aroa was his name*
> *In the immensity ...*
> *Existing alone, he became the universe ...*
> *He created the land of Hawaii.*

Carved wooden figure known as A'a, Rurutu, Austral Islands, French Polynesia (18th century).

The god is here depicted in the process of creating other gods and men: his creations cover the surface of his body in the form of 30 small figures. The main figure itself is hollow, and a removable panel on its back reveals a cavity, which originally contained 24 small figures. In 1821 a group of Rurutu islanders travelled to a London Missionary Society station on another island, where they presented this and other figures of their gods to the missionaries as a symbol of their acceptance of Christianity.

Subsequently this figure was used as an image of paganism by fund-raising missionaries in Britain. On being acquired by the British Museum, it became an icon of 'primitivism' for modernist artists such as Picasso and Henry Moore, both of whom owned replicas of it. The figure also inspired a poem by the English poet William Empson (1906–84), entitled 'Homage to the British Museum', which begins:

> *There is a Supreme God in the ethnological section;*
> *A hollow toad shape, faced with a blank shield ...*

The poem ends:

> *Let us offer our pinch of dust all to this God,*
> *And grant his reign over the entire building.*

Religions in the British Museum

This guide book follows the current layout of the British Museum, which is generally organized by cultures and continents. This offers the benefit of focus, but inevitably cannot be comprehensive. Objects associated with some world religions (such as Judaism and Sikhism) and aspects of others (including modern Christianity and Buddhism, or Islam in Pakistan, Bangladesh and Indonesia) are not currently displayed, and in some cases they are not in the collection. But what this guide can do is point out some of the evidence preserved in the Museum for the beliefs people held, how they worshipped and practised their religions (for example, how they buried their dead), and what they expected to happen thereafter. Some of these beliefs belong only to the distant past, while others have millions of followers today.

There are two especially fertile birthplaces for world religions – India and the area we now call the Middle East. This guide explores the religious art, beliefs and experience of the latter in the ancient world, and the emergence of its three major faiths: Judaism, Christianity and Islam. It also covers Asia: Hinduism, Buddhism and Jainism, Confucianism, Daoism and Shintō. Finally, we look at the diversity of beliefs and practices in the Americas, Africa and the Pacific world.

The pediment over the main entrance of the British Museum illustrates the way many 19th-century Europeans thought about religion. Humanity is seen emerging from the primeval swamp through the civilizing influence of religion. Appropriately for an entrance designed to look like a Greek temple, civilization is represented by Greek muses of the arts and sciences.

This fusion of religion with world learning was part of the Museum from its foundation in the mid-18th century by Sir Hans Sloane: as both a scientist and a confident Christian, he wanted to display what he saw as the glories of God's work. In the Enlightenment Gallery (**1**), turning right from the Great Court, you can see how Europeans began seriously to study other religions such as Buddhism. Collectors and explorers including Captain Cook began to acquire examples of religious art and practice from all over the world, and this collecting and reflecting continues today, as can be seen in the Wellcome Trust Gallery: Living and Dying (**24**), directly north of the Great Court.

Tour 1

Judaism and the Old Testament

*Leave the Great Court by the West door to **4**, Egyptian sculpture, and stop by the Rosetta Stone in the centre. To your right is the giant head of Ramesses II.*

This tour provides background to Judaism and the Old Testament, and also to early Christianity. It moves around ancient Egypt, Iraq, Israel and Palestine, and ends in Sudan and Ethiopia.

Several of the major world religions have been forged in the crucible of persecution. The Jews suffered at the hands of a succession of ancient empires: Egyptian, Assyrian, Babylonian and Roman. These empires all created colossal images and massive temples for their official religions, presided over by rulers who were also often priests. These empires and their religions have

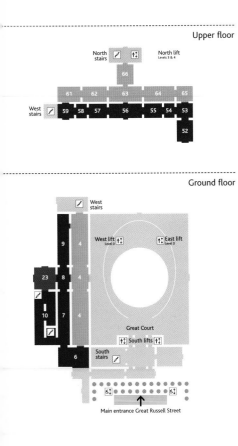

Upper floor

Ground floor

Ramesses II, Thebes, Egypt (c.1270 BC). (**4**)

	Royal graves of Ur Egyptian pyramids (2500 BC)		Ramesses II (1270 BC)	Saul (1020 BC)		Solomon (965 BC)	Assyrians conque Israel (722 BC)
3500 BC Sumer							Assyrians (950–612 BC)
		'Queen of the Night' (1792–1750 BC)	Moses (1200s BC)		David (1000 BC)		Black Obelisk (c.827 BC)
3000 BC	2000 BC				1000 BC	900 BC	

vanished: what links this tour is the faith that has survived their persecution.

Abraham, Moses and Solomon are among the names found in Judaism, Christianity and Islam. The Old Testament Book of Exodus tells the story of how Moses led the Jews out of captivity in Egypt. This is usually dated to the 15th–13th century BC, and the pharaoh is thought to be Ramesses II (1279–1213 BC).

Now turn back towards the Rosetta Stone, cross the gallery and go ahead into 23.

On your left is one of several pairs of Assyrian winged bullmen from several centuries later. This is expressive of the power of the states and religions with which the Jews had to contend in later centuries. Like the Chinese dragon, this is a mythical creature providing magical protection for the palace of a king who was also high priest of the national god, Asshur. Assyrian religion shared a common language and many gods with the Babylonians and Sumerians. There was also a strong magical element, using astrology and divination, with religion providing some certainty in an uncertain world where nature was perceived as hostile and often capricious.

left
Ashurnasirpal II
(king 884–859 BC), Assyrian
stela from Nimrud, Iraq.
(**Great Court**)

right
Colossal Assyrian winged bull
from the Palace of Sargon II,
Khorsabad, Iraq (c.710–705 BC).
(**10**)

	Nebuchadnezzar (597 BC)	Cyrus and Persians conquer Babylon (539 BC)	King Herod (40 BC)	Crucifixion of Christ (c. AD 29)	Romans destroy Jerusalem (AD 70)	Copts
	Babylonians (612–539 BC)				Roman Empire (27 BC–AD 410)	
achish siege (700 BC)	Babylonians deport Jews (587 BC)	Babylonian exile ends (538 BC)	Essenes by Dead Sea (150 BC)	Birth of Christ (4 BC)	Ethiopian Christians (AD 300) First monasteries in Egypt	
00 BC		500 BC		BC/AD		

The Taylor Prism, Assyrian, Nineveh, Iraq (694 BC). (10)

After Moses, leadership of the Jews eventually passed to David (c.1000 BC) who fought the Phillistines, and to Solomon his son. There then follows a split in the 10th century into two kingdoms: Judah in the south including Jerusalem, and Israel in the north. The next two objects relate to kings of Israel and Judah during this period.

Pass between the two winged bullmen and go left into the Lachish Room (10).

The next object is in the case on your right. The Taylor Prism records the Assyrian King Sennacherib's achievements. In 701 BC he destroyed 46 cities of the state of Judah and deported 200,150 people. He shut up Hezekiah, king of Judah, in Jerusalem 'like a caged bird'. This event is described in the Old Testament (2 Kings and Isaiah). Judah and Jerusalem eventually fell in 587 BC to the Babylonians who had conquered the Assyrians. Interestingly, the prism makes no mention of the siege of Lachish in Judah, which took place during the same campaign and is illustrated in panels from Sennacherib's palace, now also in 10. These alabaster panels decorated a room in the palace and record a ferocious siege with siege engines and ramps.

The siege and capture of the city of Lachish in 701 BC, Assyrian, Nineveh, Iraq (c.700–692 BC). (10)

Royal graves of Ur Egyptian pyramids (2500 BC)		Ramesses II (1270 BC)	Saul (1020 BC)	Solomon (965 BC)	Assyrians conque Israel (722 BC)
3500 BC Sumer					Assyrians (950–612 BC)
	'Queen of the Night' (1792–1750 BC)	Moses (1200s BC)	David (1000 BC)		Black Obelisk (c.827 BC)
3000 BC	2000 BC		1000 BC	900 BC	

*Now retrace your steps to the Rosetta Stone, in the centre of **4**, and turn right. Go to the end of the gallery and stop at another pair of winged bullmen (**6**). On your left is the Black Obelisk.*

Its relief sculptures glorify the achievements of King Shalmaneser III with scenes of tribute from Egypt, Iran, Turkey and Israel. The second register from the top includes the earliest surviving picture of an Israelite. The Biblical Jehu, king of Israel, brought or sent his tribute of silver and gold in around 841, as the inscription tells us. This relates to events described in the Old Testament Book of Kings.

*Again retrace your steps to the Rosetta Stone, and go on to the other end of **4** beyond the giant head of Ramesses. Take the West stairs. We are now going even further back in time, and will then revisit the era we have just glimpsed in greater detail.*

The Black Obelisk of Shalmaneser III (858–824 BC), Assyrian, Nimrud, Iraq (c.827 BC). (**6**) Detail of the Black Obelisk, showing the Israelites bringing tribute to the Assyrian king.

Nebuchadnezzar (597 BC)		Cyrus and Persians conquer Babylon (539 BC)	King Herod (40 BC)	Crucifixion of Christ (C. AD 29)	Romans destroy Jerusalem (AD 70)	Copts

Babylonians (612–539 BC)	Roman Empire (27 BC–AD 410)

Lachish siege (700 BC)	Babylonians deport Jews (587 BC)	Babylonian exile ends (538 BC)	Essenes by Dead Sea (150 BC)	Birth of Christ (4 BC)	Ethiopian Christians (AD 300) First monasteries in Egypt

700 BC	500 BC	BC/AD	

At the top of the West stairs (**59**) are remarkable prehistoric lime plaster statues from 'Ain Ghazal, Jordan (c.7200 BC), among the earliest large-scale representations of the body. They may represent gods or ancestors, but we will never know as there are no written sources.

Jericho is one of the world's earliest cities although by 7000 BC its population was probably only 2000. It was defended by its famous walls, associated with the much later Old Testament figure of Joshua, Jewish leader after Moses.

Jericho's dead were buried in rock-cut tombs as reconstructed in the display in **58**, or beneath the floors of houses. Sometimes the skull was removed and the features reconstructed in plaster and paint with shells for eyes. This may have been part of an ancestor cult.

In the next room (**57**) you can see evidence for the Jews' neighbours and enemies: Philistines (Goliath, as slain by David, was a Philistine), Assyrians and Babylonians. As you enter the next room (**56**), look back above the entrance at one of several fragments from the temple to Ninhursag goddess of childbirth (c.2500 BC). It comes from southern Iraq, near Ur. Now cross to the other half of the gallery.

Plastered skull, Jericho, Israel (c.7000–6000 BC). (**59**)

Royal graves of Ur Egyptian pyramids (2500 BC)		Ramesses II (1270 BC)	Saul (1020 BC)	Solomon (965 BC)	Assyrians conquer Israel (722 BC)

3500 BC Sumer   Assyrians (950–612 BC)

	'Queen of the Night' (1792–1750 BC)	Moses (1200s BC)	David (1000 BC)	Black Obelisk (c.827 BC)

3000 BC	2000 BC	1000 BC	900 BC

Abraham is traditionally regarded as the father of three world religions: Judaism, Christianity and Islam. According to the Old Testament he came from the Sumerian town of 'Ur of the Chaldees' and migrated to Canaan', the Promised Land', settling at Shechem (modern Nablus). Ur was occupied from around 5000 to 300 BC, but there is no conclusive proof that this was the city of Abraham.

Leonard Woolley excavated the 'Great Death Pit' of the Royal Cemetery at Ur. He liked biblical allusions so named this object the 'Ram in a Thicket'. In the Book of Genesis, God ordered Abraham to sacrifice his son Isaac, but at the last moment

'Abraham looked, and behold behind him a ram caught in a thicket by his horns: and Abraham went and took the ram, and offered him up for a burnt offering in the stead of his son'.

The 'Ram in a Thicket', Ur, Iraq (c.2600 BC). (**56**)

| Lachish siege (700 BC) | Babylonians deport Jews (587 BC) | | Babylonian exile ends (538 BC) | Essenes by Dead Sea (150 BC) | | Birth of Christ (4 BC) | | Ethiopian Christians (AD 300) First monasteries in Egypt |

Nebuchadnezzar (597 BC) — Cyrus and Persians conquer Babylon (539 BC) — King Herod (40 BC) — Crucifixion of Christ (c. AD 29) — Romans destroy Jerusalem (AD 70) — Copts

Babylonians (612–539 BC) — Roman Empire (27 BC–AD 410)

700 BC   500 BC   BC/AD

This 'ram' is actually a goat, and has no connection with the Biblical story. Abraham is also four centuries or so later.

Also at this end of **56** is a truly extraordinary depiction of early religion. Now known as the 'Queen of the Night' relief, it is Babylonian (1792–1750 BC) from southern Iraq (**56**, *case 23*). Originally painted red, she wears the horned headdress of a Mesopotamian deity and holds a rod and ring of justice, symbols of her divinity. She is a goddess of the underworld: her legs end in the talons of a bird of prey. She may be Ishtar, goddess of sexual love and war, her sister who ruled over the underworld, or the demoness known in the Bible as Lilith.

*Now move on into the next room (**55**), cases 1–2.*

These are symbols of the important Mesopotamian gods: the solar disc of the sun god Shamash, the crescent of the moon god Sin and the eight-

Boundary stone, Babylon (1099–1082 BC). (**55**, *cases 1–2*)

The 'Queen of the Night', reconstruction of relief, Old Babylonian, Southern Iraq (1792–1750 BC). (**56**, *case 23*)

	Royal graves of Ur Egyptian pyramids (2500 BC)	Ramesses II (1270 BC)	Saul (1020 BC)	Solomon (965 BC)	Assyrians conquer Israel (722 BC)
3500 BC Sumer					Assyrians (950–612 BC)
	'Queen of the Night' (1792–1750 BC)	Moses (1200s BC)	David (1000 BC)		Black Obelisk (c.827 BC)
3000 BC	2000 BC		1000 BC	900 BC	

pointed star of Ishtar, the triangular spade of Marduk, and the wedge-shaped stylus of Nabu, the god of writing.

At the far end of this gallery on the right are more early written documents *(case 10)*.

The Epic of Gilgamesh is a huge work in Akkadian (the language of Babylonia and Assyria). The Flood Tablet describes the meeting of Gilgamesh, legendary ruler of Uruk, with Utnapishtim. He, like Noah in the Bible, had been forewarned of a plan by the gods to send a great flood. He built a boat and loaded it with everything he could find. He survived the flood while mankind was destroyed. He released a dove and a swallow but they did not find dry land to rest on, and returned. Finally a raven that he released did not return, showing that the waters had receded.

The Assyrians had conquered Israel and deported its people in the 8th century BC. Now, in the 6th century BC, the remaining kingdom of Judah was destroyed by Babylon: 'By the rivers of Babylon – there we sat and there we wept when we remembered Zion' (Book of Psalms). When Persia in turn conquered Babylon in 539 BC the Jews were allowed to return.

The Flood Tablet, relating part of the Epic of Gilgamesh, Nineveh, Iraq (7th century BC). (**55**, *case 10*) This famous cuneiform tablet is from the library of the Assyrian King Ashurbanipal (reigned 668–627 BC).

| Lachish siege (700 BC) | Nebuchadnezzar (597 BC) | Babylonians deport Jews (587 BC) | Cyrus and Persians conquer Babylon (539 BC) | Babylonian exile ends (538 BC) | Essenes by Dead Sea (150 BC) | King Herod (40 BC) | Birth of Christ (4 BC) | Crucifixion of Christ (C. AD 29) | Romans destroy Jerusalem (AD 70) | Copts | Ethiopian Christians (AD 300) First monasteries in Egypt |

Babylonians (612–539 BC)

Roman Empire (27 BC–AD 410)

700 BC · 500 BC · BC/AD

Cylinder of Nabonidus,
Sippar, Iraq (c.555–540 BC).
(**55**, *case 12*)

*Now find the long wallcase 12
in the centre of the gallery.*

This cylinder (*left*) records
the pious reconstruction by
Nabonidus (reigned 555–539 BC)
of the temples of the moon and
sun gods. He was a successor of
Nebuchadnezzar, who imprisoned
the Jews in Babylon. His son
was Bel-shar-usur, the biblical
Belshazzar. Their nemesis was the
Persian king Cyrus.

*Now move on through **54** and **53**
then right into **52**, Ancient Iran.*

The clay cylinder in the centre
case (*below*) is an account by
Cyrus, king of Persia (559–530 BC)
of his conquest of Babylon in 539 BC
and capture of Nabonidus, the
last Babylonian king. Cyrus claims
to have achieved this with the aid
of the god Marduk. He returned

to their homelands people who
had been held in captivity in
Babylon, including the Jews. This
cylinder has been described as
the 'first charter of human rights',
but it reflects a tradition of kings
(like later politicians) beginning
with promises of reform.

These galleries reflect the
religions that were eventually
supplanted by Islam in Iraq and
Iran, Turkey and Egypt.

*At this point you may wish to
find a seat, as objects illustrating
the centuries that lead up to
Christianity are not currently
on show.*

Basalt relief showing a
storm-god, neo-Hittite,
Carchemish, Turkey
(10th century BC). (**53**)

Cyrus Cylinder, Babylon
(c.539–530 BC). (**52**)

	Royal graves of Ur Egyptian pyramids (2500 BC)		Ramesses II (1270 BC)	Saul (1020 BC)		Solomon (965 BC)		Assyrians conquer Israel (722 BC)
3500 BC Sumer							Assyrians (950–612 BC)	
		'Queen of the Night' (1792–1750 BC)	Moses (1200s BC)		David (1000 BC)		Black Obelisk (c.827 BC)	
3000 BC	2000 BC				1000 BC		900 BC	

Jews, Christians and Romans

The Jews returned from their exile 'by the rivers of Babylon' in the 6th century BC, and rebuilt the Temple in Jerusalem. Their next major threat came from the expanding Roman empire. Herod ruled as King of Judaea but, after he died in 4 BC, Judaea became a Roman province, administered by officials such as Pontius Pilate. In AD 66 the Jews revolted, but were crushed only after four years of bitter conflict. The armies of emperor Titus destroyed Jerusalem, including the Temple. The 'Wailing Wall' of that Temple survives in Jerusalem today.

Another and much more extensive Jewish Diaspora began: 'Sephardic' Jews to Spain and Portugal, 'Ashkenazi' Jews to Germany and Central Europe, and Jews throughout the Muslim world and soon throughout Asia.

Two objects from this era are described and illustrated below. (neither currently on display). Limestone chests like the one here were used by the Jews to hold the bones of the dead. The inscription states that it contains the 'bones of the family of Nicanor, the Alexandrian, who made the gates', most probably a pair of bronze gates given to the Temple of Herod in Jerusalem in 10 BC. Under King Herod of Judaea, Jerusalem was rebuilt and the Temple was completely remodelled.

Limestone ossuary, Roman/Jewish, Jerusalem (1st century BC /AD).

Nebuchadnezzar (597 BC)	Cyrus and Persians conquer Babylon (539 BC)		King Herod (40 BC)	Crucifixion of Christ (c. AD 29)	Romans destroy Jerusalem (AD 70)	Copts

Babylonians (612–539 BC)	Roman Empire (27 BC–AD 410)

Lachish siege (700 BC)	Babylonians deport Jews (587 BC)	Babylonian exile ends (538 BC)	Essenes by Dead Sea (150 BC)	Birth of Christ (4 BC)	Ethiopian Christians (AD 300) First monasteries in Egypt

700 BC	500 BC	BC/AD

This was the Jerusalem of Jesus Christ, whose life and impact on Europe and the world are explored in Tour 3. The final part of this tour stays in the ancient Middle Eastern world and looks at some of the earliest evidence for Christianity and its rivals in Egypt, Israel and Palestine, and its spread to Ethiopia.

This jar (*right*) was found at the foot of cliffs in the desolate country overlooking the Dead Sea, near the site of a monastery of extremely religious Jews, the Essenes, who had moved there c.150 BC. In 1947 an Arab goatherd stumbled into a cave here and found ancient Hebrew manuscripts, now known as the Dead Sea Scrolls, stored in cylindrical jars like this one. They are thought to have come from the library of Qumran, and include nearly all the books of the Old Testament. It was in terrain like this that the first Christian hermits and monks established themselves, especially in Egypt, away from the world of emperors and armies.

Pottery jar of the sort used to store the Dead Sea Scrolls, Qumran, Israel (1st century AD).

Royal graves of Ur Egyptian pyramids (2500 BC)		Ramesses II (1270 BC)	Saul (1020 BC)	Solomon (965 BC)	Assyrians conquer Israel (722 BC)
3500 BC Sumer					Assyrians (950–612 BC)
	'Queen of the Night' (1792–1750 BC)	Moses (1200s BC)	David (1000 BC)		Black Obelisk (c.827 BC)
3000 BC	2000 BC		1000 BC	900 BC	

Christianity in Egypt and Nubia, *Rooms 65 and 66*

To reach 65, leave 55 via 54 and turn left into 65.

In **65** and **66** you can see the beginnings of Christianity in Egypt, Nubia and Ethiopia.

The evangelist St Mark reputedly brought Christianity to Egypt, via Alexandria, home of a large Jewish community. Christianity was heavily persecuted in the 3rd century, but was widely accepted thereafter. The first monasteries are created here, beginning with hermits in rock-cut tombs. Christians in Egypt were known as Copts, from a corruption of the Greek word for Egyptians. Christianity declined in Egypt after the arrival of Islam, although there are still Coptic Christians today.

In 65 go to cases 17–18 (to the right of the door).

In the sixth century Nubia was converted to Christianity. There is evidence here also of a later 14th-century bishop from Nubia.

Now leave 65 by the other door and go through 64 and 63 and turn right into 66, Coptic Egypt.

Frieze from the cathedral at Faras, Sudan (7th century). (**65**, *case 17*) The dove or eagle beneath a Coptic-type cross represents paradise.

| Lachish siege (700 BC) | Babylonians deport Jews (587 BC) | Nebuchadnezzar (597 BC) | Babylonian exile ends (538 BC) | Cyrus and Persians conquer Babylon (539 BC) | Essenes by Dead Sea (150 BC) | King Herod (40 BC) | Birth of Christ (4 BC) | Crucifixion of Christ (c. AD 29) | Romans destroy Jerusalem (AD 70) | Copts | Ethiopian Christians (AD 300) First monasteries in Egypt |

Babylonians (612–539 BC)

Roman Empire (27 BC–AD 410)

| 700 BC | 500 BC | BC/AD |

Limestone gravestone, Coptic Egypt (8th century).

In Egypt this is the era of the first monasteries and the Desert Fathers such as St Antony. He spent 20 years in the desert withstanding the temptations famously depicted by later artists (see p.45). St Catherine's monastery in Sinai survives today.

In the wall painting below, the figures with raised arms are three saints, accompanied by an angel. Their miraculous preservation from burning was used to illustrate the Christian triumph over death. Arranged around this panel are the figures of Saints Cosmas and Damian and their brothers (all martyred by burning during the reign of the emperor Diocletian).

Ethiopia

Christianity in Ethiopia dates back to at least the 4th century, and claims descent from the son of Solomon and the Queen of Sheba, hence their emperor's title as 'lion of Judah'.

The painting illustrated opposite vividly recalls the rich pageant of religious procession in Ethiopia today. Priests carry the sacred Tabot, symbolic representation of the biblical Ark of the Covenant. This may show the festival of Epiphany or the feast day of St George, as the saint is represented. An angel in a cloud represents the Holy Spirit and the presence of God.

Wall painting of the martyrdom of saints, Wadi Sarga, Egypt (6th century). (**66**)

Royal graves of Ur Egyptian pyramids (2500 BC)	Ramesses II (1270 BC)	Saul (1020 BC)	Solomon (965 BC)	Assyrians conquer Israel (722 BC)
3500 BC Sumer				Assyrians (950–612 BC)
'Queen of the Night' (1792–1750 BC)	Moses (1200s BC)	David (1000 BC)		Black Obelisk (c.827 BC)
3000 BC	2000 BC		1000 BC	900 BC

There is more material from Ethiopia in the Sainsbury African galleries (**25**). See Tour 7.

At this point you could continue with Christianity in Tour 3 or follow the emergence of Islam in Egypt and neighbouring countries in Tour 6. To find out more about ancient Egyptian, Greek and Roman religions take Tour 2.

Painting of a religious procession, unknown artist, Ethiopia (19th century). (**66**)

Nebuchadnezzar (597 BC)	Cyrus and Persians conquer Babylon (539 BC)	King Herod (40 BC)	Crucifixion of Christ (c. AD 29)	Romans destroy Jerusalem (AD 70)	Copts	
Babylonians (612–539 BC)				Roman Empire (27 BC–AD 410)		
achish siege (700 BC)	Babylonians deport Jews (587 BC)	Babylonian exile ends (538 BC)	Essenes by Dead Sea (150 BC)	Birth of Christ (4 BC)	Ethiopian Christians (AD 300) First monasteries in Egypt	
00 BC		500 BC		BC/AD		

Tour 2
Egypt, Greece and Rome

*You can start this tour on the Upper floor by taking the stairs or lifts in the Great Court to the Upper floor, crossing the bridge and passing through **56** to **63**, then turn right into **64**.*

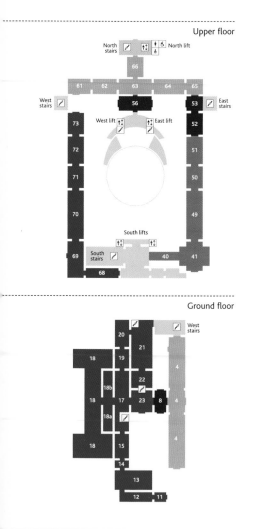

Upper floor

Ground floor

Egypt

This tour begins by looking into the commemoration of the ancient Egyptian dead, and their preservation of parts of the deceased person's body in the belief that there was an afterlife that could be enjoyed, but only if the right rituals were properly observed. These beliefs showed an extraordinary resilience over 3000 years.

In **64** you can see the beginnings of ancient Egyptian religion and massive building in honour of the gods. Ideas of the afterlife, as in most cultures, feature banquets for the virtuous and wealthy, and continued labour for nearly everyone else.

The ancient Egyptian concept of the afterlife is expressed in

opposite
Predynastic Egyptian man (3400 BC).
(**64**, *case 15*)
This man died more than 5000 years ago. Before mummification was developed around 2700 BC, bodies were placed in shallow desert graves and frequently did not decay in the hot dry sand. This body is surrounded by various kinds of grave-goods for use in the afterlife.

Pre-mummy (3400 BC)	Pyramids (2500 BC)	Akhenaten (1353 BC)
Cycladic Greece (2600 BC)		
Mummification (2700 BC)		Ramesses II (1270 BC)
3000 BC	2000 BC	1000 BC

tomb paintings such as the one below from the tomb of Nebamun, who is about to let fly a throw-stick into a mass of birds above a papyrus thicket. The hieroglyphs describe him as 'taking recreation and seeing what is good in the place of eternity'.

Shabti figures were intended to work in the afterlife on behalf of the deceased. One of the scenes on the box illustrated (*p.26*) shows Henutmehyt adoring the sons of Horus, who protected the internal organs of the deceased.

*Now return to **63** for a closer look at mummification.*

The inner coffin of Henutmehyt (*case 9*), a priestess ('Chantress of Amun'), is entirely covered in gold leaf apart from her wig, eyes and eyebrows. This lavish use of gold suggests she was a wealthy woman. Below is a kneeling figure of the sky goddess Nut, with her wings unfurled, protecting the deceased.

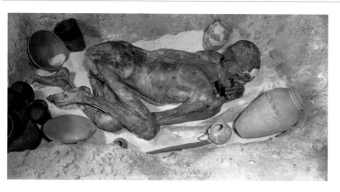

above
Nebamun fowling in the marshes, wall painting from his tomb, Thebes, Egypt, 18th Dynasty (c.1350 BC). (**61**, *reopening late 2008*)

Battle of Marathon (490 BC)

Roman Egypt (30 BC)

Constantine converts to Christianity (AD 313)

Parthenon (447 BC)

Christ (4 BC–AD 29)

Alexander the Great (336 BC)
Greeks in Egypt (332 BC)

Augustus (27 BC)

End of pagan sacrifice (AD 391)

500 BC

BC/AD

Books of the Dead (*see right*) helped the deceased to pass through the dangers of the underworld and be reborn into new life. The heart (depicted here as a pot) was believed to be the seat of the emotions, the intellect and the character. If when weighed the heart did not balance with the feather, then the dead person was condemned to non-existence, and to be devoured by the composite beast depicted here. Osiris, the most important of the Egyptian gods, is shown seated under a canopy.

Mummy case and portrait of Artemidorus, Hawara, Roman Egypt (c. AD 100–120).
(**62**, *case 22, centre, lying flat*)
A combination of a Greek personal name, a Roman-style portrait and a traditional Egyptian mummy.

left
Shabtis from the tomb of Henutmehyt, Thebes, Egypt, 19th Dynasty (c.1250 BC).
(**63**, *case 9*)

right
Inner coffin of Henutmehyt, Thebes, Egypt, 19th Dynasty (c.1250 BC). (**63**, *case 9*)

Pre-mummy (3400 BC)	Pyramids (2500 BC)	Akhenaten (1353 BC)
Cycladic Greece (2600 BC)		
Mummification (2700 BC)		Ramesses II (1270 BC)
3000 BC	2000 BC	1000 BC

Many animals were regarded as sacred to the gods and their mummies preserved in sanctuaries, including bulls, cats and even crocodiles. There are examples here in **63** (*case 10*) and **62** (*case 29*).

In **61** wall paintings from the tomb of Nebamun show his anticipated afterlife. The celebrated cat sacred to the goddess of wisdom can be seen in the Egyptian sculpture gallery (**4**) on the Ground floor.

*Take the West stairs from **61** to the Ground floor, turning right at the far end of the Egyptian sculpture gallery (**4**) if you want to trace Greek religions from prehistory. You may wish to begin with the mature temple art of the Parthenon era (**18**), in which case turn right halfway down the gallery (**4**) and go to p.29.*

left
Page from the Book of the Dead of Hunefer, Thebes, Egypt, 19th Dynasty (c.1280 BC). (**62**, *wallcase 24*)

below
Cat sacred to Bastet, goddess of wisdom, Late Period (c.664–332 BC). (**4**)

left
Faience wedjat eye, Egypt (1069–945 BC). (**62**, *case 23, opposite Books of the Dead*)
The Egyptians used amulets to protect both the living and the dead.

Battle of Marathon (490 BC)		Roman Egypt (30 BC)	Constantine converts to Christianity (AD 313)
Parthenon (447 BC)		Christ (4 BC–AD 29)	
Alexander the Great (336 BC) Greeks in Egypt (332 BC)	Augustus (27 BC)		End of pagan sacrifice (AD 391)

Marble figurine of a woman, Cyclades, prehistoric Greece (c.2700–2500 BC). (**11**, *case 3*)

Greece

*Begin in **11**.*

Cycladic figurines are usually female and naked with folded arms. Facial features were often painted in. The feet point downwards, so they could be laid down, propped up or perhaps carried. They probably had religious significance and come mostly from graves, though they may have been used by the living first. *Move on to **15**.*

By the classical Greek period there is an elaborate pantheon of gods covering most areas of life including nature, such as the sea (Poseidon), and specific places (Athena for the city of Athens). The 12 Olympian gods are presided over by Zeus and represented in Homer as having all the usual human desires and failings, rather like the gods in Wagner's opera cycle, 'The Ring'. Mortals communicated with gods through sacrifice and offerings and via oracles like the famous one at Delphi (see the end of this tour). Gods communicated with mortals through thunderbolts, sea monsters, earthquakes and showers of gold, and by spreading their protection like a cloak over the cities and heroes they favoured. There was no institutional church in the modern sense – religion and state were indivisible, as throughout the ancient world.

*Now go on to **17**, Nereid Monument, and left into **18**, Parthenon Galleries.*

Relief panel from the Tomb of Kybernis, king of Xanthos (known as the 'Harpy Tomb'), Xanthos, Turkey, Lycian (c.480 BC). (**15**) Female-headed birds carry small figures that may represent the souls of the dead.

Pre-mummy (3400 BC)	Pyramids (2500 BC)	Akhenaten (1353 BC)
	Cycladic Greece (2600 BC)	
	Mummification (2700 BC)	Ramesses II (1270 BC)
3000 BC	2000 BC	1000 BC

The Parthenon, *Room 18*

The sacred robe or peplos of Athena was escorted to the Acropolis by the procession of the Great Panathenaic Festival, held in Athens every four years. It was carried on a ship that moved on wooden rollers. These horsemen (*see below left*) are part of that procession. This frieze also probably commemorates dead heroes from the wars with the Persians, who had destroyed an earlier temple on the Acropolis.

Displayed on the wall facing the entrance to the gallery is the climax of the Parthenon frieze (*see below right*). Once the procession had climbed up on to the Acropolis, the sacred robe was dedicated to the ancient olive wood statue of Athena as guardian of the city.

On the left, a priest and a child hold the folded garment. To the right, Athena is seated on a stool, with Hephaistos the blacksmith god.

The east pediment shows the birth of the goddess Athena from the head of her father Zeus. In the two corners the time of day is represented by the chariot of Helios, god of the sun, rising at dawn, and the chariot of Selene, the moon goddess, sinking beneath the horizon. Notice the head of one of the exhausted horses that have spent the night drawing the chariot of the moon across the sky (*above*).

*Return to **17** and then go straight ahead and left into **22**, the Hellenistic world.*

Head of a horse of Selene, from the east pediment of the Parthenon. (**18**)

below left
Horsemen from the west frieze of the Parthenon, Athens (c.438–32 BC). (**18**, *this scene is just inside the entrance of 18, on the right*)

below right
The climax of the Parthenon frieze. (**18**)

Battle of Marathon (490 BC)

Roman Egypt (30 BC)

Constantine converts to Christianity (AD 313)

Parthenon (447 BC)

Christ (4 BC–AD 29)

Alexander the Great (336 BC)
Greeks in Egypt (332 BC)

Augustus (27 BC)

End of pagan sacrifice (AD 391)

500 BC

BC/AD

The Hellenistic world, *Room 22*

The Hellenistic world of the next century, in the age of Alexander the Great, extends not only around the Mediterranean including Spain and southern France, but also to Egypt and southern Russia and as far east as the Indus river, where its influence can be found in Buddhist art *(see Tour 5)*.

Look at the bronze mask of Dionysos *(case 8)*. Following Alexander the Great's conquest of Egypt, aspects of the Greek and Egyptian religions often merged. The vessel from which this mask comes was a cross between a Dionysiac wine-mixing bowl and the ritual bucket used in the worship of Isis.

right
Bronze head of a goddess, probably Aphrodite, Sadak, Turkey, Hellenistic Greek (200–100 BC). (**22**)
This statue may be of Aphrodite (goddess of love whom the Romans called Venus) or the Iranian goddess Anahita, who was later assimilated with the Greek goddesses Aphrodite and Athena.

right
Marble column drum from the later temple of Artemis at Ephesos, Turkey, Hellenistic Greek (325–300 BC). (**22**)
The messenger god Hermes, with his winged staff and wide-brimmed sun hat, appears here as leader of souls to the underworld. The woman standing in front of him may be Iphigenia, Alkestis, Eurydice or Persephone. The winged youth with a sword may personify death.

Pre-mummy (3400 BC)	Pyramids (2500 BC)	Akhenaten (1353 BC)
	Cycladic Greece (2600 BC)	
	Mummification (2700 BC)	Ramesses II (1270 BC)
3000 BC	2000 BC	1000 BC

*Now turn left and left again into the Egyptian sculpture gallery (**4**) and up the West stairs. Turn right at the top into **73–69**, the upper Greek and Roman galleries.*

Here you can see the influence of the Greeks in southern Italy (**73**), the very mixed culture of Cyprus, a crossroads of the Mediterranean (**72**), the distinctive religion of the Etruscans (**71**) and finally Rome itself (**70**).

Rome
Start with case 1.

This head once formed part of a statue of the first emperor Augustus (ruled 27 BC–AD 14). He defeated Mark Antony and Cleopatra and took possession of Egypt, which became a Roman province. Statues of Augustus were erected in Egyptian towns as far south as modern Sudan. Later this head was torn from the statue and buried beneath the steps of a local temple where it was symbolically trampled on. Other material from Meroë is displayed in **65**.

The role of chief priest of Republican Rome, the Pontifex Maximus, was assumed by Augustus, when he also initiated the worship of emperors, alive and dead. Catholic popes later took over the title Pontifex Maximus, which can still be found on inscriptions all over Rome.

opposite page
Colossal marble statue of Apollo, Cyrene, Libya, Roman (2nd century AD). (**22**) Cult statues like this one were the focus for ritual activity in temples. Apollo holds a lyre in his role as god of music. He is also the god of healing and youth, and associated with the sun. His androgyny is a common feature of religious art.

above
Cameo portrait of Augustus, Roman (c. AD 14–20). (**70**, *case 8*) He wears the aegis usually associated with the goddess Minerva. The jewelled headband was added later.

left
Bronze head of Augustus, Roman, from Meroë, Sudan (c.27–25 BC). (**70**, *case 1*)

Battle of Marathon (490 BC)	Roman Egypt (30 BC)	Constantine converts to Christianity (AD 313)
Parthenon (447 BC)	Christ (4 BC–AD 29)	
Alexander the Great (336 BC) Greeks in Egypt (332 BC)	Augustus (27 BC)	End of pagan sacrifice (AD 391)

500 BC | BC/AD

*Now move into **69** (cases 33, 32 and 12).*

Roman religion was designed to ensure success in war (through intercession by the god Mars), love (the goddess Venus) and fertility (the goddess Ceres). Ancestors were venerated as the manes. There were also domestic gods (lares) for just about everything: the god of the threshold gives his name to the month January. As in Greece, gods were entertained by games and theatricals. As the empire expanded, so did imports of exotic religions, ending with Christianity, and including the cult of Mithras from Persia. He is shown here in Eastern costume, killing a bull, the spilling of whose blood was believed to bring about the rebirth of light and life. His devotees, members of a secret male society, consumed bread and water at communal meals. This earned them the particular enmity of the Christians.

*Late pagan and early Christian Roman material is also on show in **41**. Leave **69** via **68** (Money), then cross **37** to the left and go ahead via **40** to **41**, and see first centre case 5.*

Mithras slaying the bull, marble, Roman (2nd century AD).
(69)

Pre-mummy (3400 BC)   Pyramids (2500 BC)   Akhenaten (1353 BC)

Cycladic Greece (2600 BC)

Mummification (2700 BC)   Ramesses II (1270 BC)

3000 BC   2000 BC   1000 BC

The practice of sacrifice to the Greek and Roman gods was not officially ended until AD 391, and the next object shows the strength of paganism in Rome even after this date.

This is late pagan art in Rome before the triumph of Christianity. It was probably commissioned to commemorate a former consul, a famous orator and prominent opponent of Christianity. He is shown on a wheeled carriage drawn by four elephants, his death symbolized by a draped funeral pyre. Two eagles, representing the soul, fly upwards as he is carried into heaven by winged figures that personify the winds. They pass an arc with signs of the zodiac and are watched by Helios, the sun god. At the summit five ancestors welcome his arrival and elevation to divine status, and it would be difficult to imagine it any more elaborate.

Carved ivory leaf showing apotheosis, Roman (c.400). (**41**, *centre case* 5)

left
Corbridge lanx, Roman Britain, Corbridge, Northumberland (4th century).
The scene shows the god Apollo at the entrance to a shrine, holding a bow, his lyre at his feet. His twin sister Artemis (Roman Diana), the hunter goddess, enters from the left, and the helmeted goddess is Athena (Roman Minerva). The Greek island of Delos was the birthplace of Apollo and Artemis, and Athena was also worshipped there. This shows a late flowering of Greek and Roman beliefs a very long distance from the Mediterranean, during a brief era of stability before centuries of uncertainty. (**49**)

Battle of Marathon (490 BC)	Roman Egypt (30 BC)	Constantine converts to Christianity (AD 313)
Parthenon (447 BC)	Christ (4 BC–AD 29)	
Alexander the Great (336 BC) Greeks in Egypt (332 BC)	Augustus (27 BC)	End of pagan sacrifice (AD 391)

Tour 3

Christianity

*Leave the Great Court by **1** (Enlightenment)
and turn left through the gallery to the East
stairs. At the top, turn left through **52**
(Ancient Iran) to **51**. Alternatively take the
East lift and cross the bridge to **56** then right
through **55–53** and right through **52** to **51**.*

European prehistory, Rooms 51–50

You may want to go straight on
to Christian art, or explore first
the kinds of religions that
predated it in Europe and often
continued alongside and blended
with it. Understanding the
religious beliefs and rituals of
prehistoric peoples is difficult
because they did not leave a
written record. The only direct
evidence is from archaeology,
although that can sometimes
tell us a great deal, as with
'Lindow Man'.

Upper floor

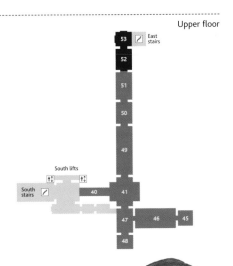

left
Seated terracotta figurine
from Vinca, Serbia
(c.4500–4000 BC). (**51**)
This was possibly a household
god, kept in a modest shrine.

right
Gold cape from Mold, Wales
(c.1900–1600 BC). (**51**)
It probably had a ceremonial
function in religious rituals.

Ethiopian Christians (300)   End of western empire (476)

Christ (c.4 BC–AD 29)   Constantine converts to Christianity (312)   Birth of Muhammad (570)

Copts in Egypt (200)   First monasteries in Egypt (323)   Sack of Rome (410)   St Benedict regulates monasticism (54...)

BC/AD   500

Celts and Romans, *Rooms 50–49*

The Romans conquered Britain at the end of the Iron Age, but are not a reliable source on its religions or the Druids. These were priests who probably carried out sacrifices to the gods, spirits and ancestors. These were everywhere (in water especially) rather than in specific buildings, and there are almost no images of them.

'Lindow Man' met a horrific death. He was struck on the top of his head twice with a heavy object, and then received a vicious blow in the back that broke one of his ribs. He was strangled and his neck broken. By now he was probably dead, but just in case his throat was cut. Finally, he was placed face down in a pond in the bog. This elaborate sequence of events suggests that his death may have been a ritual killing. He may have been a human sacrifice by Druids. He had consumed a drink containing some mistletoe pollen (sacred to the Druids) shortly before his death.

The Battersea Shield is one example of the many precious objects that have been retrieved from rivers and lakes in prehistoric Europe. Others include the Chertsey and Witham shields and the Waterloo helmet. The Welwyn Garden City burial gives a good idea of the anticipated afterlife for chiefs.

*Now continue into **49**, Roman Britain.*

left
'Lindow Man', Lindow, Cheshire (1st century AD). (**50**)

right
Battersea Shield from the River Thames (1st century BC). (**50**)

Christianity began as an exotic import from the East alongside many other cults in the Roman empire *(see Tour 2)*. Britain has some of the earliest evidence of Christian art. The Hinton St Mary mosaic is the earliest securely dated head of Christ, identifiable as such by the Greek letters X and P, Chi and Ro, the first letters of his name.

Christ is shown as a Roman emperor, and to either side are pomegranates, symbols of eternal life from ancient Greece. The old pagan beliefs were here juxtaposed with the new.

Objects from Water Newton are the earliest Christian church silver. Precious objects like these were buried in the expectation of a retrieval that never happened. After the collapse of Roman power in northern Europe, Christianity hung on precariously in Britain.

top
Christian silver from Water Newton, Cambridgeshire (4th century). (**49**)

above
Head of Christ from the Hinton St Mary mosaic, Dorset (4th century). (**49**)

right
Wall painting showing Christians at prayer, from Lullingstone, Kent (4th century). (**49**)

Ethiopian Christians (300)

End of western empire (476)

Christ (c.4 BC–AD 29)

Constantine converts to Christianity (312)

Birth of Muhammad (570)

Copts in Egypt (200) First monasteries in Egypt (323) Sack of Rome (410) St Benedict regulates monasticism (52)

Christian Europe, *Room 41*

Christianity had begun shakily as an outlawed religion. The emperor Constantine converted to Christianity in 312, and it was now tolerated, becoming the state religion from 391. However, during the 5th–10th centuries it came under attack again.

Rome and the western empire fell to barbarian armies and took centuries to recover, but Christianity flourished in the eastern capital Constantinople and throughout Byzantium, the eastern Roman empire, for the next thousand years. The eastern and western churches diverged formally after 1054 into the western 'Catholic' and the eastern 'Orthodox' church. The Greek and Russian Orthodox churches still acknowledge the Patriarch of Constantinople as their ultimate Head.

Meanwhile in Britain Christianity had survived in Scotland and Ireland *(see cases 26–28)*, but needed a 6th-century missionary, St Augustine, to re-establish it in England. The Sutton Hoo burial *(cases 48, etc)* is that of a pagan Saxon king who was converted to Christianity. Pagan and Christian beliefs also sit side by side on the Franks Casket *(centre case 41)*.

This is the era of the Lindisfarne Gospels (British Library) and Book of Kells (Dublin). Under King Alfred England just survived the onslaught of the Vikings, who are eventually converted *(cases 30–31)*.

above
Ivory panel showing an archangel, from Constantinople (Istanbul) (6th century). (**41**, *case 8*) This is the largest surviving Byzantine ivory panel.

below right
The Fuller Brooch, Anglo-Saxon (late 9th century). (**41**, *case 36*) This depiction of the five senses was probably designed for liturgical use.

far left
Gold-glass medallion, probably from the catacombs, Rome (4th century). (**41**, *case 1, no 28*) At this stage Christianity is still literally an underground movement in Rome. The small figure of Christ presides over this wedding scene.

The life of Christ in medieval art, *Rooms 40–41*

*(Room **40** reopens in 2008)*

left: Virgin and Child, ivory, France (14th century). (**40**)
A tender scene of mother and son, typical of Gothic ivories at their most elegant.

below: The Magi offer Christ their gifts, from the Franks Casket, whalebone, Northumbria, Anglo-Saxon (8th century). (**41**, *centre case 41*)
Other scenes come from ancient Rome (Romulus and Remus), Judaism (the capture of Jerusalem by the emperor Titus in AD 70) and pagan Germany (Wayland the Smith).

bottom: The childhood of Christ, ceramic tiles from Tring (14th century). (**40**)
Christ is here shown performing miracles, from the popular lives not found in the gospels.

Ethiopian Christians (300)	End of western empire (476)

Christ (c.4 BC–AD 29)   Constantine converts to Christianity (312)   Birth of Muhammad (570)

Copts in Egypt (200)   First monasteries in Egypt (323)   Sack of Rome (410)   St Benedict regulates monasticism (529)

left: The Baptism of Christ, Anglo-Saxon ivory, England (late 10th–early 11th century). (**41**, *case 35, no. 24*)
A bearded and unusually elegant John the Baptist here baptizes his cousin Jesus in the River Jordan.

below: The Crucifixion, panel from an ivory casket, Roman (5th century). (**41**, *case 5, no. 5*)
This is the earliest known narrative portrayal of the Crucifixion. Christ gazes at us, triumphant in death, identified by the inscription as 'King of the Jews'. Mary and John stand to the left. Judas hangs at the extreme left, with a spilled sack of coins at his feet.

bottom: The Resurrection, alabaster, English (late 14th century). (**40**)
Christ steps triumphantly from a tomb that is guarded by moustachioed Roman soldiers in medieval armour. English alabasters survive all over Europe from Iceland to Croatia. Scenes like this were re-enacted in cycles of mystery plays in towns like Chester and York, where they are still performed today by amateur actors.

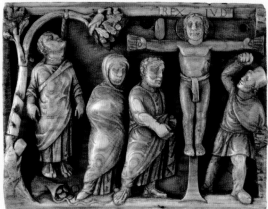

utton Hoo (c.625)   Viking attacks begin (790)   Chartres cathedral (1154)   Martin Luther (1517)
Charlemagne (800)

Lindisfarne Gospels (700)   Book of Kells (800)   Fall of Byzantium (1453)

Russian Orthodox church (988)   Great Schism (1054)   Franciscan order (1210)   Henry VIII breaks with Rome (1534)
First Crusade (1096)   Westminster Abbey (1270)

1000   1500

Icons, *Room 40*

(Room 40 reopens in 2008)

Icons, from the Greek word for image, became a standard part of devotion in the Byzantine and Orthodox churches. They might form a screen or iconostasis in a church, or be for private devotion.

top
Icon of St Peter, Constantinople (Istanbul), Byzantine (c.1320). (**40**)
This was discovered under layers of whitewash and varnish on the back of a later icon. The scroll exhorts us 'to abstain from the passions of the flesh that wage war against your soul'. This is a world-weary St Peter, with deeply-lined eyes, later to be claimed as first Pope and founder of the Church in Rome, where he was martyred.

right
Icon of St John the Baptist, Constantinople (Istanbul), Byzantine (c.1300). (**40**)
In this compelling painting, St John gazes directly at us with a sense of wisdom and serenity. The inscription identifies him as 'the Forerunner'.

Ethiopian Christians (300)   End of western empire (476)

Christ (c.4 BC–AD 29)   Constantine converts to Christianity (312)   Birth of Muhammad (570)

Copts in Egypt (200)   First monasteries in Egypt (323)   Sack of Rome (410)   St Benedict regulates monasticism (529)

BC/AD

left
Icon of Triumph of Orthodoxy,
Constantinople (Istanbul), Byzantine
(c.1400). **(40)**
This portrays the annual Festival of
Orthodoxy celebrated in Lent. The icon
of the Virgin Mary, seen here, was the
most famous icon of Constantinople. The
Evangelist St Luke was thought to have
painted it, making it an actual life
portrait of the Virgin. The empress
Theodora and her young son appear on
the left.

right
Icon of St George, Pskov, north-western
Russia, Byzantine (late 14th century). **(40)**
Evangelists such as Sts Cyril and Methodius
brought Christianity and the Cyrillic alphabet
to the Slavs in the 9th century. Greek and
Russian Orthodox Christianity both survived
the Fall of Byzantium in 1453.
In this early masterpiece of Russian painting
the saint reins in his leaping horse as he kills
the dragon.

Itton Hoo (c.625)	Viking attacks begin (790)	Chartres cathedral (1154)	Martin Luther (1517)
	Charlemagne (800)		
Lindisfarne Gospels (700)	Book of Kells (800)		Fall of Byzantium (1453)
	Russian Orthodox	Great Schism (1054)	Franciscan order (1210)	Henry VIII breaks
	church (988)	First Crusade (1096)	Westminster Abbey (1270)	with Rome (1534)

1000   1500

Relics and saints, *Rooms 40 and 45*
(*Room **40** reopens in 2008*)

Relics played an essential part in
the development and spread of
Christianity as of Buddhism.
You can now see reliquaries and
depictions of one early Christian
martyr and one medieval one.

top
Reliquary of St Eustace, Basle, Switzerland (c.1210). (**40**)
According to legend, Eustace was a general under the
emperor Trajan, and was converted to Christianity while
hunting, after seeing a vision of a stag with a crucifix
between its antlers. He was burnt to death with his wife
and sons. This reliquary contained fragments of a skull.

middle
Enamel cross, France or Belgium, Romanesque
(12th century). (**40**)
Panels from the back of this cross relate the legend of
the discovery of the True Cross by Constantine's mother,
St Helena. The Old Testament scenes on the front refer to
the Crucifixion symbolically. This was probably designed
to hold one of many relics of the True Cross.

bottom
Winged seraph, painting from the Palace of
Westminster (1260s). (**40**)
Westminster Abbey became the coronation
church as well as the shrine of Edward the
Confessor. The adjoining palace is now the
site of the Houses of Parliament. This and
other paintings here survived the fire
of 1834, and give a small idea of what has
been lost from pre-Reformation England.

Ethiopian Christians (300)

End of western empire (476)

Christ (c.4 BC–AD 29)

Constantine converts to Christianity (312)

Birth of Muhammad (570)

Copts in Egypt (200)   First monasteries in Egypt (323)   Sack of Rome (410)

St Benedict regulates monasticism (529)

BC/AD

right
The Holy Thorn Reliquary of Jean, Duc de Berri, Paris (c.1400–10).
(**45**, *central case*)
This reliquary was made to house a relic of the Crown of Thorns,
placed on the head of Christ at his crucifixion. A dramatic scene of
the Last Judgement surrounds the relic, featuring the Virgin Mary, St
John the Baptist, Christ and the twelve Apostles with God the
Father at the top. At the bottom, four angels sound trumpets as the
dead emerge from their tombs. Behind the figure of God is a gold
relief of the Holy Face on the cloth of St Veronica, a fragment of
which may have been contained here.

below
Alabaster panel with the Martyrdom of St Thomas Becket, English
(c.1450–1500). (**40**)
This alabaster panel shows Thomas Becket, 12th-century Archbishop
of Canterbury, kneeling in prayer. Knights approach and attack him
with swords. They acted on a misunderstood instruction from King
Henry II who was in dispute with Becket. Canterbury rapidly
became a popular place for pilgrimage, as described in Chaucer's
14th-century 'Canterbury Tales'.

To reach **45**, leave **40** via **41**,
turn right into **47** and then left
through **46**.

Sutton Hoo (c.625)	Viking attacks begin (790)		Chartres cathedral (1154)	Martin Luther (1517)
	Charlemagne (800)			
Lindisfarne Gospels (700)	Book of Kells (800)			Fall of Byzantium (1453)
		Russian Orthodox church (988)	Great Schism (1054) First Crusade (1096)	Franciscan order (1210) Westminster Abbey (1270)	Henry VIII breaks with Rome (1534)
		1000		1500

The Reformation era,
Rooms 45–46

The leaders of the Protestant Reformation, like many religious leaders, were seeking to restore an earlier simplicity to an existing faith that had in their view become corrupt. The proliferation of relics was one of many aspects of the Catholic Church criticised by reformer Martin Luther, who in 1517 nailed a list of 95 grievances (including indulgences) on the church door in Wittenberg, Germany. Indulgences, being sold to let people off years of purgatory, were partly fundraising for the very expensive St Peter's in Rome. Appropriately, in the island cases around the Holy Thorn reliquary (**45**) there are images both of Luther (*case 3, no. 14*) and of John of Leyden, leader of the Munster Anabaptists, an extreme Protestant group (*case 5, no. 5*). In the next room (**46**) in *case 5* on the right are further images of the leaders of Protestantism (Erasmus, Luther and Zwingli) and their Catholic Habsburg opponents. Henry VIII of England was one of several rulers to support the Reformation (*see case 6*).

Tilman Riemenschneider, Adoration of the Magi, limewood panel, southern Germany (c.1505–10). (**40**)
This panel was adapted from an engraving by Martin Schongauer. Riemenschneider (1460–1531) was one of the last Gothic sculptors in southern Germany.

Ethiopian Christians (300)

End of western empire (476)

Christ (c.4 BC–AD 29)

Constantine converts to Christianity (312)

Birth of Muhammad (570)

Copts in Egypt (200)   First monasteries in Egypt (323)   Sack of Rome (410)

St Benedict regulates monasticism (529)

These images, from the Museum's prints and drawings collection, give an idea of the range of religious art and commentary produced during the 15th and 16th centuries.

top
Martin Schongauer, The Temptation of St Antony, engraving, Germany (1470s).
St Antony was one of the founders of monasticism in the Egyptian desert *(see pp.21–2)*.

left
Albrecht Dürer, The Four Horsemen of the Apocalypse, woodcut, Germany (1498).
This is based on St John's visions from the Book of Revelation. The first rider with a bow represents pestilence. The second, with a raised sword, represents war. The third, with the empty scales, represents famine. In front rides Death, sweeping citizens and a king into the jaws of Hades. For a modern interpretation of this subject from Mexico see Tour 7 and p.47.

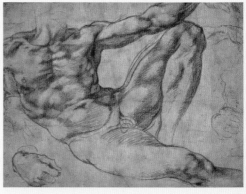

right
Michelangelo Buonarotti, Study for Adam, drawing, Italy (c.1510–11).
This beautiful red chalk life drawing of a male nude is for the figure of Adam painted on the ceiling of the Sistine Chapel, Rome. He stretches out to receive life from God.

| ton Hoo (c.625) | Viking attacks begin (790) Charlemagne (800) | | Chartres cathedral (1154) | Martin Luther (1517) |

Lindisfarne Gospels (700) — Book of Kells (800) — Fall of Byzantium (1453)

Russian Orthodox church (988) — Great Schism (1054) First Crusade (1096) — Franciscan order (1210) Westminster Abbey (1270) — Henry VIII breaks with Rome (1534)

1000 — 1500

Christianity also followed the flag with explorers and colonists in the Americas, Asia and Africa. In **46**, *wallcase 15* shows the beginnings of the Portuguese, Spanish, Dutch and British Empires. For them, as the Habsburg medal says, 'One world is not enough.'

In the bottom of this case is a reminder of a traditional arena for religious devotion: a model of the Holy Sepulchre in Jerusalem.

Protestant Europe fused Humanist and Enlightenment ideals and art forms with Christian beliefs. Leading scientists like Isaac Newton were devout Christians as was the founder of this Museum, Hans Sloane, who wanted its combination of natural and manmade curiosities to show the work of God across continents and centuries. Christian faith inspired reformers of slavery, prisons and mental health facilities in 18th-century England, as well as missionary work worldwide. A medal from the Society for the Abolition of the Slave Trade founded in 1787 (**46**, *case 18, no. 17*) shows a chained slave with the inscription: 'Am I not a man and a brother?'

Slavery was eventually abolished in British territories in 1833.

The Portland Font, gold, England (1797). (**47**, *case 1*)

	Ethiopian Christians (300)		End of western empire (476)
Christ (c.4 BC–AD 29)	Constantine converts to Christianity (312)		Birth of Muhammad (570)
	Copts in Egypt (200) First monasteries in Egypt (323)	Sack of Rome (410)	St Benedict regulates monasticism (52

Now go on into **47** which shows (on your left) the growing European interest in other religions and their arts, such as Islam. On your right is a miniature gold font (*opposite*).

The Baroque and neo-classical revival of Roman architecture is reflected in cathedrals such as St Peter's, Rome and St Paul's, London and in objects like this. Faith, Hope and Charity preside over the lavish font (*case 1*) designed for the christening of a duke's grandson. Both were likely to be depicted as Romans on their tombs.

Some of the impact of missionaries and the art they took with them all over the world can be seen in **24**, Living and Dying, on the Ground floor (*see Tour 7*). The Mexican Day of the Dead festival is an adaptation of All Saints and All Souls Days in November; the papier mâché figures of the horsemen derive from Dürer's depictions of the Horsemen of the Apocalypse. Carnival, the festival that precedes Lent and abstinence before Easter, is given an unusual spin by the Andean miners of Bolivia. The wallcase 'Praying for Health', behind the Bolivian display, shows the continuation of an ancient tradition in Italy and southern Germany of leaving images of body parts in thanks for cures, a practice observed at the shrines of medieval saints.

Day of the Dead figures, papier mâché, Linares Brothers, Mexico (1980s). **(24)**

Tour 4

Hinduism and Jainism

*Begin in the Great Court and go north past the bookshop and through **24**, Living and Dying, to the North stairs and straight ahead into **33**, the Hotung Gallery. Turn to your left to begin in the South and Southeast Asian section of the gallery.*

Asia is the birthplace of Hinduism and Buddhism, Jainism and Sikhism, Confucianism, Daoism and Shintō, among others. On this tour it is possible to see traditional Hindu and Jain art. Paintings are not on permanent display (for conservation reasons), so some are illustrated here, particularly to give a sense of the colour and context that is now missing from the sculpture.

Hinduism

The roots of what we now call Hinduism go back to the ancient civilization of the Indus Valley (3000–2000 BC) *(see case 3 on your left)*. The first of the sacred texts of Hinduism, the Rig Veda, dates from c.900 BC. Most of the

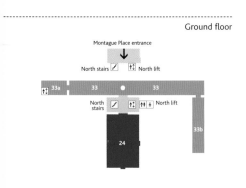

Ground floor

Montague Place entrance

North stairs   North lift

33a   33   33

North stairs   North lift

33b

24

Painting of the temple of Jagannatha (a form of Krishna) at Puri, Orissa (late 19th century). *(see p.54)*

Lao-tzu born (c.605 BC)   Mahavira born (c.54

Indus Valley culture (c.3000–2000 BC)   Buddha (c.563–483 BC)

Rig Veda completed (c.900 BC)   Confucius born (c.551 BC)

3000 BC   2000 BC   1000 BC

sculpture here dates from much later, from c. AD 1000 onwards.

On arriving at a temple dedicated to Shiva you see the elephant-headed figure of Ganesha, god of good beginnings and good luck, and remover of obstacles. In the next bay on your left (*between cases 7 and 10*) is a typical example. Like all this stone sculpture, it was originally brightly coloured, as in the painting illustrated below.

Parvati, left alone by the god Shiva, her consort, created Ganesha. Shiva, on his eventual return, was stopped from entering the house by Ganesha, who didn't know who he was. Shiva, quick to anger, knocked off his head and then replaced it with that of an elephant to soothe the distraught Parvati.

Ganesha has one tusk, either because he used the other one as a pen (he is god of writing) or because he tore it off and threw it at the moon when it laughed at him. There are often many different explanations in Hindu myth. Ganesha is fond of food, as you can see here, and so Hindus make food offerings to him, such as melted butter, rice, fruit and sweets. Like many Hindu and Buddhist deities he is multi-armed to show enhanced powers, usually represented by symbols in each hand. This reaches a climax in Tibetan Buddhist art.

Now turn to the centre of this part of the gallery and the dancing figure of Shiva.

Painting of Ganesha, Punjab Hills (c.1720). He is holding an axe and elephant goad, and is seated on a lotus.

mperor Ashoka (273 BC)   Buddhism in China (65)   Buddhism state religion of Japan (685)   Chola art (c.900–)   Mughals conquer India (1526)

Spread of Buddhism to SE Asia (1st century AD)

Gandharan art (1st century BC–)   Buddhism in Tibet (645)   Diamond Sutra (868)   Angkor Wat, Khmer temple (1152)

BC/AD   1000

The ultimate aim of every Hindu is to obtain liberation (moksha) from constant cycles of birth and death. In order to achieve this, Hindus must work hard and live a righteous life. They are brought up to respect gods, elders and ancestors, and all living creatures.

Bronzes like this from the Chola period are extraordinarily expressive and informative, addressed to a mainly illiterate audience, as was medieval Christian art, and still arresting for us today. Shiva presides over the beginning and end of each cycle of time: he beats his little drum in one hand to begin, and ignites the flame in the other for the destruction that is eventually necessary to purge the world of sin. He dances within an arch of flame, trampling the bovine figure of ignorance and evil underfoot. His headdress is like the mountain peak where he lives, and the waters of the Ganges with its goddess tumble down the long strands of his hair. This image was carried on poles that were inserted through the holes in the base, so it is three-dimensional.

Small Shiva shrine, sandstone, North India (18th century). (**33**, *between cases 22 and 24*)

left
Bronze figure of Shiva Nataraja (c.1100). (**33**, *centre case 37*)

right
Nandi, the white, humped bull mount of Shiva, garlanded and decorated with bells, granite (16th century). Nandi ('rejoicing') looks devotedly towards his master, ready to carry him wherever he goes.

Lao-tzu born (c.605 BC)   Mahavira born (c.54

Indus Valley culture (c.3000–2000 BC)

Buddha (c.563–483 BC)

Rig Veda completed (c.900 BC)

Confucius born (c.551 BC)

3000 BC   2000 BC   1000 BC

Behind the bronze of Shiva is the Hindu equivalent of an altarpiece, showing both Shiva and his consort Parvati. Shiva's bull Nandi and Parvati's lion are parked at their feet. A tiny Ganesha appears bottom right, while a heavenly dance band floats overhead. The painting (*below*) helps to imagine how it might look in a temple.

Go beyond the previous sculpture to the next bay on the left. Facing the window (*between cases 25 and 27, behind a Ganesha*) is this graphic depiction of Durga on the warpath. Hindu goddesses take many forms: Parvati is a role model for the mostly understanding housewife and mother. As Durga, on the other hand, she is a warrior, succeeding in ridding the world of evil where all the male gods had failed. In this case, evil is a demon disguised as a buffalo. He appears from its severed neck. Durga kills him, armed with arrows, sword and trident, as her lion bites his leg. Durga's victory is celebrated in Bengal each year, when large clay images are immersed in rivers after the festival.

Durga kills the buffalo demon, Orissa (13th century). (**33**)

Painting of Shiva and Parvati seated on a terrace, Jaipur (c.1800).

| Emperor Ashoka (273 BC) | Buddhism in China (65) | Buddhism state religion of Japan (685) | Chola art (c.900–) | Mughals conquer India (1526) |

Spread of Buddhism to SE Asia (1st century AD)

Gandharan art (1st century BC–) | Buddhism in Tibet (645) | Diamond Sutra (868) | Angkor Wat, Khmer temple (1152)

BC/AD   1000

Chamunda, sandstone, Orissa (8th–9th century). (**33**)

Even more disturbing is the goddess as Kali and Chamunda (*see behind Durga to the left*). Seated on a corpse and garlanded with skulls, she terrifies the enemies of the faithful. Her power is shown by the weapons with which she fights back the demons of ignorance and ego. After the battle with the buffalo demon, Durga became so enraged that Kali, black and with fangs, burst out from her forehead. The riverside steps or ghats where Kali was worshipped with offerings of animal blood gave their name to Calcutta (Kolkota).

Now turn back towards the dancing Shiva in the centre. On your right between cases 19 and 21 is this image of Vishnu.

Vishnu, unlike Shiva, takes many forms. His character is also unlike the mercurial Shiva, and he is known as the 'preserver'. He steps in when things go wrong, as in this depiction of him saving Manu and the sacred Vedas from an imminent flood by telling Manu to build a boat and collect together animals and seeds. When the all-engulfing flood comes, he tows the boat to safety so life can begin again, as the waters subside.

left
Painting of Durga by Kapuri Devi, Bihar (20th century).

right
Vishnu as the fish, Matsya, sandstone (9th–10th century). (**33**, *next to case 21*)

Now look up at the wall above the cases for images of Vishnu as the boar, and also behind the Chamunda you saw earlier. When the whole world was flooded, the earth was trapped underwater by a sea-demon. Vishnu, in the form of a boar, dived down into the ocean and rescued the earth, depicted as a goddess.

Now move to the other side of the gallery, between cases 34 and 35, for Vishnu as the man-lion.

Vishnu here cunningly penetrates the magic protection around an evil king, who is safe by day or night, from man or beast, indoors or outdoors. Vishnu waits till sunset disguised as a man-lion on the veranda of the palace – and then pounces!

Sculpture of Vishnu as the man-lion, Narasinha, Tamil Nadu (c.950). (**33**, *between cases 34–35*)

left
Painting of Vishnu as the boar, Varaha, rescuing the earth from the oceans, Punjab Hills (c.1740).

¬peror Ashoka (273 BC)	Buddhism in China (65)	Buddhism state religion of Japan (685)	Chola art (c.900–)		Mughals conquer India (1526)
	Spread of Buddhism to SE Asia (1st century AD)				
Gandharan art (1st century BC–)		Buddhism in Tibet (645)	Diamond Sutra (868)	Angkor Wat, Khmer temple (1152)	
	BC/AD			1000	

The Ramayana is an epic poem composed over several centuries BC and AD. Rama's wife Sita is abducted by the ten-headed demon Ravana. Rama, with the help of bears and monkeys, notably their king Hanuman, saves Sita by killing Ravana, as depicted here. Rama is seen as the model ruler and virtuous man. There is an ivory of Ravana in *case 35*.

Today Vishnu is probably most familiar as Krishna, a much-indulged child god who becomes a seductive flute player and dark-skinned lover of milkmaids, and eventually a wise king.

The giant festival carts created for his temple of Jagannatha at Puri *(see p.48)* have given us the word 'juggernaut'. A major Hindu festival today such as the Kumbh Mela can attract millions of devotees. It is held every twelve years near Allahabad at the confluence of the rivers Ganges and Yamuna.

At this point you may want to cross the gallery to look at Jain art (cases 19–21): see opposite.

Vishnu's many forms appear together in *case 10* on your right as you return to the centre of the gallery. An image of Brahma is on your left between *cases 36–39*. Brahma is the stabilizing force in Hinduism between the forces of Shiva and Vishnu. He is all-seeing, with four heads representing also the four Vedas, the key early religious texts.

left
Painting of Rama on the shoulders of Hanuman as he kills Ravana (c.1820).

right
Jagat Singh I worships Krishna (c.1700).
A painting from Rajasthan.

Lao-tzu born (c.605 BC)   Mahavira born (c.5

Indus Valley culture (c.3000–2000 BC)

Buddha (c.563–483 BC)

Rig Veda completed (c.900 BC)

Confucius born (c.551 BC)

3000 BC   2000 BC   1000 BC

J A I N S *(cases 19–21)*

Tirthankaras (ford makers) show how to cross the river of life from suffering and pain to happiness and perfect knowledge on the other shore. They are also called Jinas or conquerors, because they have conquered and controlled their desires and attained a state of inner enlightenment.

Jain art depicts the bodies of its saints as naked, smooth and slender, with the ascetic's matted hair piled on top. Mahavira (on the right here) was an Indian contemporary of the Buddha in the 6th century BC; like the Buddha he is restoring a true, ancient faith rather than instigating a new one. He too renounced the world and lived the life of a wandering holy man. His followers are vegetarian, avoid killing any living being, and are often craftsmen and traders since they cannot be farmers. Strict Jains sweep carefully, strain drinking water and wear masks to avoid killing small insects.

Some monks are naked, 'sky-clad', without any possessions at all. Today there are fewer than three million Jains in India, but many live abroad in cities such as Leicester in the UK.

To continue with Buddhism and other Asian religions in this gallery, see Tour 5.

Two Jain *tirthankaras*, schist stone, Orissa (11th–12th century). (**33**, *case 19*)

Emperor Ashoka (273 BC)   Buddhism in China (65)   Buddhism state religion of Japan (685)   Chola art (c.900–)   Mughals conquer India (1526)

Spread of Buddhism to SE Asia (1st century AD)

Gandharan art (1st century BC–)   Buddhism in Tibet (645)   Diamond Sutra (868)   Angkor Wat, Khmer temple (1152)

BC/AD   1000

Tour 5
Buddhism

Leave the Great Court by the north exit, past the bookshop, through **24**, Living and Dying, and then up the stairs straight ahead into **33**, the Hotung Gallery. Turn left and look for this sculpture (below) behind the standing Buddha in the centre of the gallery.

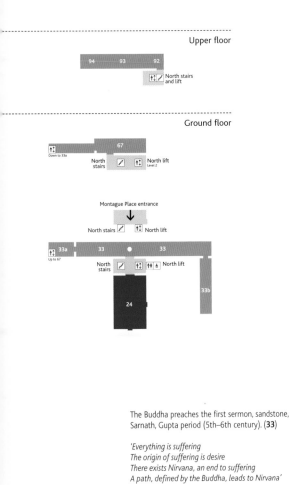

Buddhism, *Room 33*

Buddhism began as a reform movement within Hinduism, seeking to simplify practice, belief and art. The Buddha himself was not depicted until centuries later. This sculpture comes from the place where he preached his first sermon, in the deer park at Sarnath. This is a calm, uncluttered image, in contrast with much Hindu and later Buddhist art. When he renounced his princely life the 'Buddha to be' removed his heavy gold earrings, but his ear lobes were already distended, and this is shown, along with the curls on his shaved head, and the topknot that represents his wisdom. Hands communicate through a vocabulary of gestures.

The Buddha preaches the first sermon, sandstone, Sarnath, Gupta period (5th–6th century). (**33**)

'Everything is suffering
The origin of suffering is desire
There exists Nirvana, an end to suffering
A path, defined by the Buddha, leads to Nirvana'

Lao-tzu born (c.605 BC)   Mahavira born (c.540 BC)

Indus Valley culture (c.3000–2000 BC)

Buddha (c.563–483 BC)

Rig Veda completed (c.900 BC)

Confucius born (c.551 BC)

3000 BC   2000 BC   1000 BC

THE LIFE OF THE BUDDHA

The historical Buddha was born as a prince named Siddhartha Gautama in the kingdom of the Shakyas in northern India (probably in c.563 BC). In Sanskrit he is called Shakyamuni ('sage of the Shakyas').

The top-right panel shown here depicts the sleeping Queen Maya, his mother. In a dream she saw a white elephant enter her side. On the panel to the left astrologers interpret this dream. The bottom-right scene shows Maya, holding on to the branch of a tree, giving birth from her right side. The baby is depicted symbolically as a long cloth.

Siddhartha's idyllic princely life was interrupted at the age of 19, when he went outside his palace and saw the 'four sights': an old man, a sick man, a corpse and an ascetic. He left the palace to seek a way out of this world and its sufferings. He unsuccessfully tried different Hindu teachers. He then pursued physical hardships to such an extent that he reached the emaciated state seen here, when he was close to death. He then realized that the true nature of the world and the answers that he was seeking did not lie in the extremes of either the palace or complete deprivation. Instead, he set out on a more moderate path of meditation and moral conduct, the 'Middle Way', that led him to nirvana (liberation from the world).

top
Maya gives birth to the Buddha, from the Amaravati stupa (2nd century AD). (**33a**, *right-hand end of the central wall towards the window*)

above
The Buddha fasting, grey schist, Gandhara (2nd–3rd century AD). (**33**, *case 11*)

left
Death of the Buddha, grey schist panel from Gandhara (2nd–3rd century AD). (**33**, *case 13*)

right
Standing Buddha Shakyamuni, gilt bronze, post-Gupta period (7th century AD). BM/V&A. This type of Buddha was copied throughout Asia.

Relics and pilgrims

At the core of a domed stupa is
a relic of the Buddha or his
followers, as for example the
Buddha's tooth venerated in
Candy, Sri Lanka. This casket from
Afghanistan *(case 18)* probably
contained parts of his body.
He is shown with characteristic
Gandharan topknot between the
Hindu gods Indra and Brahma,
both wearing Greek-style clothes.

Between *cases 11* and *13* is
a figure from one of the most
important stupas, that at Sanchi.

The beams across stupa
gateways were held up by
bracket figures representing
female tree spirits called *yakshis*,
who were said to usher in the
spring by coaxing a tree trunk
into life.

above
Gold reliquary, set with garnets,
from a stupa at Bimaran,
Afghanistan (1st century AD).
(**33**, *case 18*)

right
Yakshi, female tree spirit,
sandstone, from a stupa at Sanchi
(1st century AD). (**33**)

Lao-tzu born (c.605 BC)   Mahavira born (c.540

Indus Valley culture (c.3000–2000 BC)   Buddha (c.563–483 BC)

Rig Veda completed (c.900 BC)   Confucius born (c.551 BC)

3000 BC   2000 BC   1000 BC

*Now go to the end of this half of the gallery, where sculptures from the remarkable stupa at Amaravati are displayed behind a glass screen (**33a**).*

Its lavish decoration reflects the wealth of this part of east-central India from foreign trade, including with the Roman world.

Pilgrims don't go inside a stupa but process around it, leaving the offerings they are shown buying here to left and right. At the entrance the Buddha waits to greet the devout. Fragments of similar lions and columns can be seen here in the gallery, as well as scenes from the Buddha's life.

Early Buddhist art represents him through symbols such as his feet, the stupa or the wheel of the Buddhist law (seen here on the soles of the feet), his throne or the tree under which he preached. One of the physical features of a Buddha is having toes the same length. Buddhist swastikas (from *svasti* meaning 'all is well') also decorate the Buddha's feet.

Symbol of the Buddha's feet, limestone slab from the Amaravati stupa (1st century BC). (**33a**, *on the end wall to the right of the entrance*)

below left
Limestone drum slab from the Amaravati stupa (3rd century AD). (**33a**)

below right
Reconstruction drawing of the stupa at Amaravati.

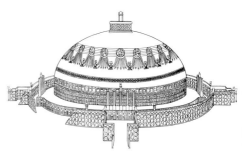

mperor Ashoka (273 BC)	Buddhism in China (65)	Buddhism state religion of Japan (685)	Chola art (c.900–)		Mughals conquer India (1526)
	Spread of Buddhism to SE Asia (1st century AD)				
Gandharan art (1st century BC–)		Buddhism in Tibet (645)	Diamond Sutra (868)		Angkor Wat, Khmer temple (1152)

Thailand, Nepal and Tibet

Now make your way back towards the centre of the gallery.

The spread of Buddhism across Southeast Asia can be traced in cases here for Sri Lanka, Java (including the epic temple of Borobudur), Cambodia, Burma, Vietnam and Thailand (*case 47*).

The three-dimensional walking Buddha (*below right*) is an invention of Thai metal sculptors, and suggests his accessibility. Here the Buddha's hand is raised in reassurance, and his left foot has almost left the ground. This is an image of the Buddha as a monk rather than a god or king, walking among the people.

Between *cases 51–52* is this Nepalese bronze (*below left*) of a Bodhisattva, who has reached enlightenment and could leave the world behind but continues to look compassionately on its sufferings and to lead souls to salvation.

In Tibet the Dalai Lama is believed to be an incarnation of Avalokiteshvara. In the 8th century Buddhist monks were invited to Tibet and eventually Buddhism took a strong hold

left
The Bodhisattva
Avalokiteshvara, gilt bronze,
Nepal (16th century).
(**33**, *by case 51*)

right
Walking Buddha, bronze,
Thailand (14th century).
(**33**, *case 47*)

Lao-tzu born (c.605 BC)   Mahavira born (c.54

Indus Valley culture (c.3000–2000 BC)   Buddha (c.563–483 BC)

Rig Veda completed (c.900 BC)   Confucius born (c.551 BC)

3000 BC   2000 BC   1000 BC

there, absorbing the native cults. The functions of king and spiritual leader were combined in the Dalai Lama. Later, Chinese emperors became enthusiastic supporters of Tibetan Buddhism.

Tibetan Buddhism combines Mahayana, Tantric and Shamanic forms. Painted on the wooden shrine in *case 53* are some of the many Buddhas, Bodhisattvas and saints in the Vajrayana or Tantric form of Buddhism. On the insides of the doors are offerings symbolizing wealth. At the centre is the Buddha with Tara, and a group of lamas. Below is the bull-headed Bhairava with multiple arms and heads, the main deity of the Yellow Hat School of lamas, which has dominated Tibetan Buddhism since the 17th century.

Painted textile (thangka) from Tibet (19th century).
A ferocious monster grasps the wheel of life – the endless series of reincarnations to which the soul is prone. The cock, snake and pig at its core represent greed, anger and ignorance – the creatures of desire and therefore creators of suffering. The Buddha stands outside this wheel of suffering at top right. By following his example we are encouraged to discipline our lives and thoughts so we are no longer deluded by the world in which we physically live.

Painted wooden shrine from Tibet (19th century). (**33**, *case 53*)

Emperor Ashoka (273 BC)	Buddhism in China (65)	Buddhism state religion of Japan (685)	Chola art (c.900–)	Mughals conquer India (1526)

Spread of Buddhism to SE Asia (1st century AD)

Gandharan art (1st century BC–)	Buddhism in Tibet (645)	Diamond Sutra (868)	Angkor Wat, Khmer temple (1152)

Sri Lanka and Burma

The Boddhisattva Avalokiteshvara looked down on the suffering in the world below and wept a lake of tears. From a lotus stem growing up from the lake emerged the figure of Tara, whose compassionate nature is beautifully expressed here. This image is one of the finest bronzes from Asia and was originally inlaid with precious stones. Buddhism arrived in Sri Lanka in the 3rd century BC and has a continuous history on the island to this day.

Now turn to the centre of the gallery facing the entrance.

'To be Burmese is to be Buddhist' goes the saying, and this has been increasingly the case since the 5th century. This Buddha is seated in the lotus position with legs crossed and holds a myrobalan, a small fruit with medicinal properties. This image was made using the dry lacquer technique, and given a modern throne recently.

left
Tara, gilt bronze, Sri Lanka (7th–8th century). (**33**)

right
Enthroned Buddha, gilded lacquer, Burma (c.1800) with throne (1994). (**33**)

China before Buddhism

Now cross the centre of the gallery to look at religions in China.

In the centuries BC elaborate rituals developed venerating ancestors and gods, using special bronze objects for food and wine. Terracotta and other ceramic figures replaced actual human sacrifices. You can see part of such a tomb group ahead of you in *case 47*.

On your left in *case 51* are examples of Chinese popular religion, which often combined with the main philosophies of Confucianism, Daoism and Buddhism.

Two major philosophies pre-date Buddhism in China. Confucianism was the official religion, and the Confucian Classics became the basis of study for all scholars and officials, with their emphasis on virtue and learning, and respect for rulers, elders and tradition. Confucius was born in c. 551 BC, but it was only much later that his thoughts were published. Confucianism still pervades Asia today.

Daoism advocated freedom in nature, and encouraged mystical practices. It stressed the need to retire from the world and master the dao or 'way'. Daoists also practiced dietary, breathing and sexual exercises, and sought immortality.

In *case 32* a 15th-century shrine model includes Laozi, its most famous philosopher.

Bronze figure of Liu Hai, god of wealth, Qing dynasty, China (1723). (**33**, *by case 51*)

left
Group of ceramic tomb figures, Tang dynasty, China (AD 700–750). (**33**, *case 47 centre*)

right
Portrait of a Confucian scholar, Korea (18th–19th century). (**67**, *case 16*) (*See p.67*)

mperor Ashoka (273 BC)	Buddhism in China (65)	Buddhism state religion of Japan (685)	Chola art (c.900–)	Mughals conquer India (1526)

Spread of Buddhism to SE Asia (1st century AD)

Gandharan art (1st century BC–)	Buddhism in Tibet (645)	Diamond Sutra (868)	Angkor Wat, Khmer temple (1152)

BC/AD   1000

Although these beliefs often overlap they were also in competition, and Buddhism suffered many purges as a result of being the newcomer, once the appeal of the exotic had worn off.

Buddhism came to China in the Ist century AD. Early evidence is displayed in *case 2* on the right at the end of the gallery. In the centre are a remarkable group of ceramic figures and a fragment of a wall painting.

Buddhism brought the concept of hell to China, and this proved a useful tool for social control as well as spiritual guidance. Purgatory was just as bureaucratic as any other aspect of life: the file was inspected with your life's deeds recorded on it, and then you were dragged to hell and its boiling vats of oil and other punishments, or accompanied to paradise by a figure like the one on the right of the gallery here. Once you arrived in the Buddhist nirvana or Western Paradise you would be greeted by Bodhisattvas, as shown in the wall painting at the back.

A luohan was a disciple of the Buddha, had magical powers and could stay alive indefinitely to preserve the Buddha's teachings. They were depicted with strongly characterized features. Note the luohan's robe: it has the patchwork worn by monks as a sign of humility.

Ceramic figure of an assistant to a judge of hell, Ming dynasty, China (16th century). (**33**)

left
Ceramic figure of a luohan, Liao dinasty, China (10th–12th century). (**33**)

right
Shakyamuni, gilt-bronze, Ming dynasty, China (early 15th century). (**33**, *to the right of the luohan in the centre of the wallcase*)

The gilt-bronze figure of the Buddha (*opposite below right*) sits on a double lotus throne, with a mandorla behind pierced with fire and floral scrolls. He has just warded off temptation, gaining peace and truth, and is shown calling the earth to bear witness to his struggles

Central Asia

Sit in front of the 15th-century wall painting of three Bodhisattvas (from the 'Pure Coolness' temple, Hebei). These illustrations are part of a remarkable cache from the Buddhist cave-temples at Dunhuang on the Silk Road, in Central Asia. They were sealed up during a period of major disturbances and recovered nearly 1,000 years later by Aurel Stein and other explorers in the early 20th century. For conservation reasons, they are not on permanent display. The earliest dated printing in the world, the Diamond Sutra (AD 868) also from Dunhuang, is on display in the British Library.

The cave-temples along the Silk Road were notable also for their giant sculptures, of the kind found until recently in Afghanistan at Bamiyan. An impressive example from China can be seen on the stairs outside this gallery.

Vaishravana, guardian of the North, riding across the waters, painting on silk, from Dunhuang, Five Dynasties period, China (mid-10th century).

left
The Buddha preaching at the Vulture Peak, embroidery on cloth faced with silk, from Dunhuang, Tang dynasty, China (8th century).

right
Bodhisattva, guide of souls, ink and colours on silk, from Dunhuang, Tang dynasty, China (9th century).

mperor Ashoka (273 BC)	Buddhism in China (65)	Buddhism state religion of Japan (685)	Chola art (c.900–)	Mughals conquer India (1526)
	Spread of Buddhism to SE Asia (1st century AD)			
Gandharan art (1st century BC–)	Buddhism in Tibet (645)	Diamond Sutra (868)	Angkor Wat, Khmer temple (1152)	

Now leave the Gallery by the central doors and continue up the North stairs and stop on the first landing to look at this colossal figure, nearly 6 metres high.

The right hand would have been raised, palm outwards in the gesture of reassurance, and the left hand lowered in the gesture of liberality. Amitabha presides over the Western Paradise, and was to become the focus for a major Amida cult in Japan (*see p.69*).

The compassionate Bodhisattva, behind you in the case, is known as Guanyin in China. The tradition of large wooden Buddhist sculpture was later adopted with dramatic effect in Japan.

below
Avalokiteshvara (Guanyin), polychromed wood, China (11th–12th century).
(**North stairs**)

right
The Buddha Amitabha from Chongguang Temple, China, white marble (6th century).
(**North stairs**)

Lao-tzu born (c.605 BC)   Mahavira born (c.54

Indus Valley culture (c.3000–2000 BC)

Buddha (c.563–483 BC)

Rig Veda completed (c.900 BC)

Confucius born (c.551 BC)

3000 BC   2000 BC   1000 BC

Korea, *Room 67*

*At the third landing on the North stairs, turn right into the Korea Foundation Gallery (**67**)*

Korea first adopted Buddhism as a state religion in AD 372, and it remained so until the last Korean dynasty, the Choson (1392–1910), reverted to Confucianism. Buddhism had a profound impact on Korean culture, and its elegant sculptures in turn influenced Japanese art when Buddhism arrived there from Korea.

There are guardians for each of the four directions, found particularly at the entrance to Buddhist temples. This one guards the east and plays a lute; the colours are an auspicious combination of red and green. Compare this painting with the guardian of the North from Dunhuang on p.65.

The frontispiece of a paradise scene *(case 7)* was painted and written in silver and gold by a monk-scribe for his mother. The Buddha is shown teaching, surrounded by crowned and bejewelled Bodhisattvas representing the Mahayana ('Greater Vehicle') tradition, while behind arhats (who have reached enlightenment) embody the Hinayana or Theravada 'tradition of the elders'. An exquisite and rare lacquer box to hold sutras such as these is also in this case.

*Continue to the top of the North stairs for Japan (**92–94**).*

below left
Guardian king, from a Buddhist temple, Korea (1796–1820).
(**67**, *far wall*)

below right
Amitabha Sutra, manuscript in 16 folds, gold and silver paint on blue paper, Korea (1341).
(**67**, *case 7*)

mperor Ashoka (273 BC)	Buddhism in China (65)	Buddhism state religion of Japan (685)	Chola art (c.900–)	Mughals conquer India (1526)

Spread of Buddhism to SE Asia (1st century AD)

Gandharan art (1st century BC–)	Buddhism in Tibet (645)	Diamond Sutra (868)	Angkor Wat, Khmer temple (1152)

Japan, *Rooms 92–94*

Shintō

Shintō, the indigenous religion of Japan, is the way of the kami, the powers of nature who are present everywhere but especially on mountains such as Fuji and at other sacred places. For nearly a century until 1945 a new state Shinto replaced Buddhism as the officially favoured religion, reinforcing the divine origin of the emperor as descended from the sun goddess Amaterasu. Shrines are marked by torii gates, at which mouths are rinsed and hands washed before entering the temple itself.

The shrine at Futamigaura, near Ise, depicted on this lacquer box, is one of the holiest shrines. Its torii gateway overlooks the sea where the famous 'twin rocks' are situated, bound together by a sacred rope – a symbol of the bonds between Nature and Humanity.

Buddhism

Buddhism reached Japan from China via Korea in the 500s. Buddhist art in Japan combines the subtlety and refinement of Chinese and Korean Buddhist art with their more ferocious aspects, closer to Buddhism's Indian roots. It developed alongside Shintō, and religions such as that of the native Ainu.

The Buddha Amida was the principal deity in temples of the True Pure Land sect, often forming the central element of a triad, flanked by two Bodhisattvas. Here (*opposite*

Shintō shrine on a lacquer writing-box, Japan (16th century).
(92–94)

Lao-tzu born (c.605 BC)   Mahavira born (c.54█

Indus Valley culture (c.3000–2000 BC)   Buddha (c.563–483 BC)

Rig Veda completed (c.900 BC)   Confucius born (c.551 BC)

3000 BC   2000 BC   1000 BC

right), Amida holds his hands in a gesture that welcomes the souls of the faithful to the Pure Land (*see p.66*).

Shaka (as Shakyamuni, the Buddha-to-be, is known in Japan) undertook six years of fasting and hardship as part of his search for the truth about existence and escape from suffering (*see p.57*). As a result he became emaciated and according to tradition his skin turned black. This small gilded bronze statue (*below*) with its layer of dull black lacquer shows him in this state. It was commissioned by the abbot of a temple and consecrated in 1630, on the day on which the death of the Buddha is commemorated.

Samurai warriors in particular followed the precepts of Zen Buddhism, introduced from China in the 12th century. Zen preached a simplicity close to nature, rather like Daoism, but with a discipline of mind and body, based on simple meditation rather than ritual.

left
The Buddha fasting, gilded and lacquered bronze, Japan (17th century). (**92–94**)

right
Buddha Amitabha (Amida in Japan), lacquered wood, Japan (13th century). (**92–94**)

| mperor Ashoka (273 BC) | Buddhism in China (65) | Buddhism state religion of Japan (685) | Chola art (c.900–) | Mughals conquer India (1526) |

Spread of Buddhism to SE Asia (1st century AD)

| Gandharan art (1st century BC–) | Buddhism in Tibet (645) | Diamond Sutra (868) | Angkor Wat, Khmer temple (1152) |

BC/AD   1000

Tour 6
Islam

*From the Great Court go north, straight ahead and down the stairs towards the Montague Place entrance. On the right is the John Addis Islamic Gallery (**34**).*

You might wish to sit down and read this first section.

Ground floor

Montague Place entrance

34

North lift
Level -1

North stairs   North lift

24

This tour begins in the deserts and caravan cities of south Arabia and rapidly spreads like Islam itself in all directions: to Egypt and Syria; to Iraq and Iran; North Africa, Spain and Sicily; via Central Asia to what are now India, Pakistan and Bangladesh; and then via Turkey into Eastern Europe. It ends in Africa.

Mecca (now in Saudi Arabia) was already a religious as well as trading centre when Muhammad was born there according to tradition in 570. From the age of 40 he began to experience revelations, and even during his life he had become lawgiver, judge and commander-in-chief as

Muhammad born (570)		Dome of the Rock (691)		Islam in Central Asia (732)
		Moors in Spain and France (700s)		Arabs in Sicily (800s)
Muhammad dies (632)	Jerusalem taken (638)	Great Mosque, Damascus (715)		Ibn Tulun mosque, Cairo (8

500   700   800

well as prophet. Muhammad saw himself as the last and greatest in a long line of prophets stretching back to Abraham. He rejected polytheism and preached that all would be judged before God regardless of wealth and status.

Islam means 'submitting oneself to the will of Allah (God)'. The Five Pillars of Islam are: accepting that there is no God but Allah, and that Muhammad is his messenger; prayer towards Mecca five times a day; fasting during Ramadan between sunrise and sunset; almsgiving; and performing the pilgrimage to Mecca, the Haj. The square Ka'ba at the centre of the shrine at Mecca predates Islam and is associated with Abraham.

It is familiar today draped in black silk as the focus for pilgrimage and daily devotion by Muslims worldwide.

The Holy Book of Islam, the Qur'an (Koran) consists of the revelations received by Muhammad, and written down in Arabic by his followers in the 7th century. There is an example just inside the gallery on the right.

Islam spread rapidly after Muhammad's death in 632. The caliphs took over Byzantine lands such as Syria and Egypt. Jerusalem fell in 638, Afghanistan in 664 and much of Central Asia by 732.

The Caliphs in Baghdad were Sunni, believing Muhammad did not designate an heir and that therefore central authority

The archangel Gabriel, from The Wonders of Creation and the Oddities of Existence, Egypt/Syria (c.1400).
Gabriel is an important figure to Muslims, as to Christians. In both traditions, Gabriel brings the Annunciation to Mary that she will give birth to Jesus. In Islam, Gabriel acts as God's messenger to the Prophet Muhammad, bringing him the words of the Qur'an. Gabriel also accompanied Muhammad on his Night Journey, bringing him from Mecca to Jerusalem through Hell and Heaven, and finally to the throne of God, in the course of one night.

Islam in sub-Saharan Africa (1070)   Safavids in Iran (1499)

Crusades (1090s)

Al-Azhar university, Cairo (988)   Ottomans capture Constantinople (1453)   Mughal empire in India (1526)

00   1000   1500

wasn't hereditary. The Fatimids in Egypt on the other hand were followers of the descendants of Muhammad's son in law, 'Ali. They are known as Shi'a Muslims. These divisions continue today. Shi'ism is the state religion of Iran and is strong in Iraq. Most Muslims today are Sunni, across the Gulf, in Turkey, Afghanistan and Pakistan, Egypt and Syria.

After two centuries of leadership by caliphs, religious authority in Islam passed to the Islamic scholars, the 'ulama. Despite rivalries and wars, there developed over the centuries an extraordinary common cultural and trading area from Africa to Asia. The stranglehold of Arabs over trade with Asia particularly in spices inspired the European age of expansion. Christianity, Europe and Islam have always been inextricably linked.

Begin with case 2, facing you as you enter the gallery.

This lamp has the lines from the Qur'an, 'The believer in the mosque is like the fish in the water, and the false believer is like the bird in a cage.'

Muhammad made the night journey with the angel Gabriel to the Rock on the Temple Mount and there they ascended to heaven. It is also where in Jewish tradition Abraham offered his son Isaac as sacrifice to God, where the Ark of the Covenant came to rest and where successive temples were built.

Mosque lamp, ceramic, made at Iznik, Turkey, for the Dome of the Rock, Jerusalem, Ottoman (1549). (**34**, *case 2*)

Muhammad born (570)   Dome of the Rock (691)   Islam in Central Asia (732)

Moors in Spain and France (700s)   Arabs in Sicily (800s)

Muhammad dies (632)   Jerusalem taken (638)   Great Mosque, Damascus (715)   Ibn Tulun mosque, Cairo

500   700   800

Egypt and Syria

The splendour of Cairo soon eclipsed that of its rivals. Cairo has the oldest university in the world, founded in 988, and has remained the major cultural focus for the Arab world.

Also in *case 2*, this panel (*below*) would have been at the head of a cenotaph placed around the grave. The inscription has verses from the Qur'an: In the Name of God, the Merciful, the Compassionate, Say: 'He is God, One, God, the everlasting Refuge, who has not begotten, and has not been begotten, and equal to Him is not anyone.'

Now go down the steps past the jar-stand and ahead to case 19, 'mosque lamps', and on your left find case 20.

Many lamps were commissioned in large numbers for the splendid mosques built in Cairo by the Mamluk Sultans and their amirs. Many are inscribed with verses from the Qur'an: 'God is the Light of the heavens and the earth; the likeness of His Light is as a niche wherein is a lamp.' The lamp (*above*) is decorated with the name and titles of the donor, and his heraldic device incorporating a red cup. A small inner container held the oil and wick.

The Crusades, beginning in 1095, were partly prompted by the capture of Jerusalem by the Seljuk Turks in 1071 and the disruption of pilgrim traffic as a result.

Glass mosque lamp, gilded and enamelled, Egypt (c.1400). (**34**, *case 20 bottom shelf*)

below left
Marble panel from a cenotaph, with inscription in Kufic script, Cairo (967). (**34**, *case 2*)

below right
Jar-stand, Egypt, Fatimid dynasty (12th century). (**34**, *at the left of the steps down into the main part of the gallery*)
A porous jug sitting on this stand filtered pure drinking water into the basin. Ritual ablutions are also obligatory before prayer.

Islam in sub-Saharan Africa (1070)

Safavids in Iran (1499)

Crusades (1090s)

Al-Azhar university, Cairo (988)

Ottomans capture Constantinople (1453)

Mughal empire in India (1526)

1000

1500

The shape of this bottle (*left*) is that of the leather water flasks used by medieval pilgrims. It was probably made for sale to them in the Holy Land, as a container for their mementoes.

Now move towards the steps and centre case 14.

Iran

Islam in Iran supplanted Zoroastrianism. Some Zoroastrians emigrated to India where they are known as Parsees (Persians) and are still found today, as also in East Africa.

This bowl (*right*) is a stunning example of Islamic art at its simplest. The inscription reads: 'He who speaks, his speech is silver, but silence is a ruby.'

These four tiles (*below*) from Iran are part of a longer frieze with an inscription written in Kufic script. It reads: 'in the name of God the most merciful, the most compassionate, there is no god but Him, the all-powerful, the all-ruling.' Rich decoration using texts like this is a feature of Islamic art, rather than a depicting of gods, prophets and events as in other world religions. The human figure is not forbidden in Islamic art, but in

Pilgrim bottle, gilded and enamelled glass, Egypt/Syria (late 13th century). (**34**, *centre case 19*)

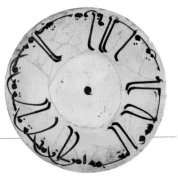

Earthenware bowl with Kufic inscription, Nishapur, Iran (10th century). (**34**, *case 14*)

Illustre-painted ceramic tiles, from Kashan, Iran (13th–14th century). (**34**, *wall near entrance*)

Muhammad born (570)   Dome of the Rock (691)   Islam in Central Asia (732)

Moors in Spain and France (700s)   Arabs in Sicily (800s)

Muhammad dies (632)   Jerusalem taken (638)   Great Mosque, Damascus (715)   Ibn Tulun mosque, Cairo

the hadith or sayings of the Prophet Muhammad it is stated that it is the role of god, not man, to create living things. Hence representations of the human form or of animals are not found in religious contexts.

Now move down the gallery on your right to cases 24–25 for pottery and tiles from Kashan and elsewhere. They give some idea of the colourful decoration of mosques and palaces.

From the late 15th century three great empires dominated the Islamic world: Ottoman Turkey, Mughal India and Safavid Iran, with which we begin *(cases 26, 36–40)*.

In Iran Shi'a Islam supported national identity against hostile Sunni powers such as Ottoman Turkey. Standards like these were carried in religious processions and also into battle. These bear the names of Muhammad and 'Ali his son in law, and are Shi'a emblems. They were carried at the Muharram ceremony, which commemorates the martyrdom of Muhammad's grandson in 680.

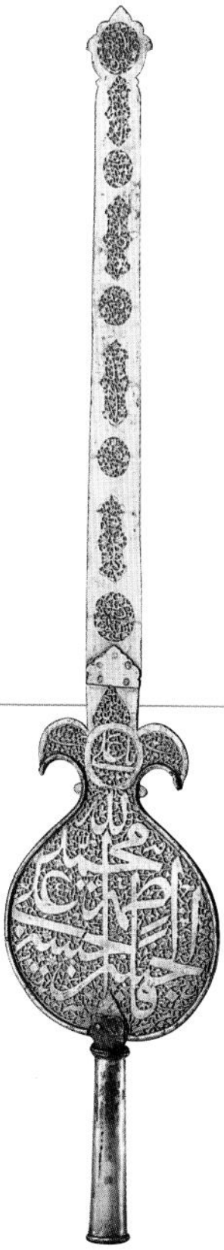

Brass standard, Iran, Safavid dynasty (17th–18th century). (**34**, *case 37*)

Islam in sub-Saharan Africa (1070)

Safavids in Iran (1499)

Crusades (1090s)

Al-Azhar university, Cairo (988)

Ottomans capture Constantinople (1453)

Mughal empire in India (1526)

1000

1500

Many Old Testament and Jewish stories were incorporated into the Qur'an: Solomon appears as not only a great and wealthy king with magical powers, but also a prophet of God. Believing that the Queen of Sheba worshipped the sun, Solomon wrote to her, to come to him 'in humble submission'.

Ottoman Turkey

Now cross the gallery to cases 27–34.

The Christian Byzantine capital, Constantinople, fell to the Ottoman armies in 1453. The Byzantine church of Hagia Sofia was transformed into a mosque. Such mosques also provided medicine, education and soup kitchens.

At its greatest the Ottoman Empire embraced the Mediterranean from North Africa round to the Balkans and the gates of Vienna. Habsburg Europe only repulsed the Ottoman armies with great effort, to avoid the same fate as Byzantium. Many traces survive from this era: strong coffee, croissants and bathhouses, as in Budapest where there are also many turban-capped tombstones like the one here (*opposite case 33*). The Ottoman Sultans controlled all three of the holiest cities of Islam, Mecca, Medina and Jerusalem. Süleyman the Magnificent (reigned 1520–66)

The Queen of Sheba (Bilqis), drawing, Iran, Safavid dynasty (16th century). This drawing depicts the moment when the hoopoe bird delivers the letter.

Muhammad born (570) Dome of the Rock (691) Islam in Central Asia (732)

Moors in Spain and France (700s) Arabs in Sicily (800s)

Muhammad dies (632) Jerusalem taken (638) Great Mosque, Damascus (715) Ibn Tulun mosque, Cairo

ordered the refurbishment of the Dome of the Rock in Jerusalem. The interior was decorated with fine hanging lamps such as the example seen earlier *(case 2)*.

Regular changing exhibitions of paintings, drawings and calligraphy are shown in the central area of this gallery.

Now cross the carpet to the other side, to the left of case 40.

Mughal India *(cases 42–43, 47)*

Today South Asia has one of the largest concentrations of Muslims in the world. Muslims began to settle there in large numbers after the capture of Delhi in 1192: you can see inscriptions from 15th-century Bengal here, on the wall to the left of *case 40*. The Mughal dynasty from Central Asia began to establish itself under Babur from the 1520s. They ruled a predominantly Hindu country, and there were many overlaps in art as well as practice. The Mughal emperor Akbar (ruled 1556–1605) attempted a synthesis of religions, in discussions with Muslims, Hindus, Jains, Parsees and Sikhs. Sikhism was founded by Guru Nanak in the early 16th century, combining elements of both Hinduism and Islam. Akbar also invited Jesuits from Portuguese Goa *(see case 47)*. His later successor Aurangzeb (died 1707), last of the great emperors, however, asserted Islam to the exclusion of all else.

top right
Brass lamp on a stand, Ottoman, made in Istanbul, Turkey (1541–5). Commissioned for the mosque of Sultan Süleyman on the island of Benefshe (modern Monemvasia), off the coast of Greece, where the Christian islanders were allowed to leave, and their church was then turned into a mosque. (**34**, *case 28*)

right
Decorated footed basin, Ottoman, Iznik, Turkey (c.1550–60). (**34**, *case 27*)

This painting comes from a massive project commissioned by the young Akbar. The Hamzanama ('Book of Hamza') is a heroic romance about the legendary adventures of the Prophet Muhammad's uncle, Amir Hamza. Here he is shown being rescued by the prophet Elijah, known to Muslims as Ilyas. Stylistically this is Persian, with some European influence, but the landscape is purely Indian, with lush jungle and peacocks.

Now move along the end wall to the left.

Islam in Europe (*case 35*)

The Moors entered Spain in AD 711 and penetrated France as far as the Loire valley until they were repulsed. They controlled Andalus (southern Spain) until the fall of Granada in 1492. Cordoba now has a 16th-century cathedral inside a former mosque founded in the 8th century on the site of a Roman temple and a Visigothic church. The merging of art styles is known as hispano-moresque; you can also see it in the European context in **46**.

The prophet Elijah rescuing Hamza's nephew, painting, Mughal India (late 16th century).

Muhammad born (570) Dome of the Rock (691) Islam in Central Asia (732)

Moors in Spain and France (700s) Arabs in Sicily (800s)

Muhammad dies (632) Jerusalem taken (638) Great Mosque, Damascus (715) Ibn Tulun mosque, Ca[

500 700 800

In medicine, maths and astronomy, medieval Europe owed a great debt to Islamic centres of learning for keeping ancient Greek knowledge alive.

The Islamic tradition of lustred earthenware was introduced into Europe through Islamic Spain. By around 1400 Christian Valencia had become the major centre of production: large quantities were exported to Italy.

Islam also established itself in Malta and Sicily. Even after Christians had regained Sicily from the Arabs, the Norman King Roger (1130) encouraged a cosmopolitan mix of Greek Orthodox, Roman Catholics, Muslims and Jews, speaking Arabic, Greek and Latin, French, Spanish, Italian, Berber and even Norse. Roger is depicted on the mosaics of Palermo and Monreale as Latin king, Byzantine emperor and Islamic caliph.

Now turn round and find the wallcase of coins (case 44).
To the right is a changing display of modern calligraphy.

The Medici Valencian vase, Valencia, Spain (c.1465–92). (**46**, *case 1*)

Islam in sub-Saharan Africa (1070)   Safavids in Iran (1499)

Crusades (1090s)

Al-Azhar university, Cairo (988)   Ottomans capture Constantinople (1453)   Mughal empire in India (1526)

900   1000   1500

Islam in art today

Many traditional elements of Islamic art have been re-invigorated by modern artists.

'Ali Omar Ermes (born in Libya 1945 and now living in London) uses quotations from classical Arabic poetry, including a poem by an Abbasid caliph commenting on the injustice of society and its lack of concern for the poor.

Ceramics by Tunisian artist Khalid Ben Slimane (*case 6*) are at the top of the steps on your left as you leave the gallery.

*Go back towards the Great Court, via **24**, and then down at the far end into the Sainsbury African Galleries (**25**). Go right at the entrance to the gallery into the far room for the textiles case.*

Having spread rapidly along the north coast from Egypt to Morocco after Muhammad's death, Islam penetrated south into the Sahara, through the caravan trade.

There are usually examples of African textiles on display here with Islamic motifs and texts. At the other extreme end of these galleries are ceramics

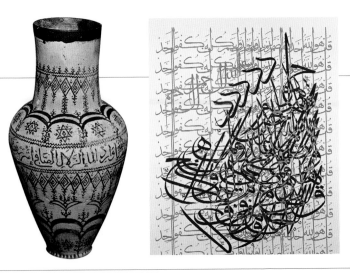

left
Tunisian water pot (19th century). (**25**, *case 20 bottom shelf*)

right
Contemporary calligraphy, Ahmed Mustafa (1983).

Muhammad born (570)	Dome of the Rock (691)	Islam in Central Asia (732)	
	Moors in Spain and France (700s)		Arabs in Sicily (800s)
Muhammad dies (632)	Jerusalem taken (638)	Great Mosque, Damascus (715)	Ibn Tulun mosque, Cairo (82

and metalwork. Tunisian Nja Mahdaoui has decorated a drum with calligraphic forms, and Algerian Rachid Koraichi has paid tribute to a great Sufi mystic with a series of calligraphic sculptures.

Hand of Fatima stickers, Cairo (1990s). Stickers are placed on car windscreens, in the home and work place. The inscription is from the Qur'an, 'oh God, gracious to his servants'.

Detail of cotton sheet with drawn and painted magical designs of Islamic inspiration, Asante, Ghana (1951).

Tour 7
Africa, the Americas and the

This tour looks at ancient as well as pre-industrial and contemporary cultures, some displayed by culture and others thematically in the Wellcome Trust Gallery (24), where it begins. Leave the Great Court by the north exit behind the bookshop.

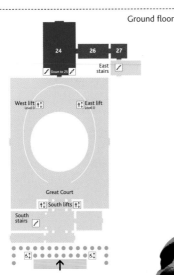

Ground floor

Lower floor

left
Hoa Hakananai'a, Easter Island (Rapa Nui), Polynesia (c. AD 1400). (24)

right
Kalabari ancestral screen, Nigeria (19th century). (25, case 13)

Ancestors

Begin with the Easter Island statue facing you as you enter from the Great Court.

Easter Island is famous for its stone statues of human figures, known as moai, which stood on stone platforms. They were probably carved to commemorate important ancestors and were made from around AD 1000 until the 17th century. With the adoption of Christianity in the 1860s, the remaining standing moai were toppled.

Now go downstairs into the Sainsbury African galleries (25) and turn to your left in the first section (Woodcarving) and the right-hand case.

Maya (200 BC–AD 1000)

Incas (1200–1534)   Aztecs (1325–1521)

Easter Island head (1400)

200 BC   BC/AD   1000

Pacific world

Kuba kings from the Congo were commemorated by ndop, not actual portraits but idealized images. The emblem of this king, founder of the ruling dynasty, is a board game, mancala. These portraits helped to ensure the spiritual continuity of kingship from one generation to the next. In the same case are Shona headrests from Zimbabwe, used mainly by men who are said to be visiting their ancestors during sleep.

Now turn back towards the entrance and the end wall of this section.

The Kalabari of the Niger delta were important middlemen in the trade between the interior of West Africa and Europe. Their clan-based trading houses became wealthy from the Atlantic slave trade in which they were middlemen. They commemorated their deceased leaders with screens which served as shrines to communicate with their spirits. This example (*opposite below right*) shows a house-head in his masquerade outfit ('white man's ship on head'). Screens were kept in the headquarters of the trading company and offerings (especially of gin) were made to them at least once a week. Keeping ancestors happy with food and drink is a feature of many cultures.

Now turn back to your right, to case 14.

Carvings like this double-headed dog were used in rituals

Wooden carving of King Shyaam aMbul aNgoong, Kuba-Bushoong, Democratic Republic of Congo (18th century). (**25**, *case 12*)

Kozo, the double-headed dog, Democratic Republic of Congo (19th century). (**25**, *case 14*)

First African slaves in America (1518)		Kalabari screen (1800s)	'Scramble for Africa' (1880s)
Spanish in America (1519–34)		Captain Cook in the Pacific (1770s)	Decolonization (1945–)
Benin mask (1500)		Kuba ancestor (1700s)	Kongo dog (1900)
1500		1700	1900

Ivory salt-cellar, Benin, Nigeria (16th century). The Virgin Mary and the infant Jesus are here combined with snakes and hunting scenes in an object designed to appeal to Portuguese traders in West Africa.

to solve problems or to gain wealth. An iron blade is driven into this figure to make a wish or a curse. Dogs are considered as mediators between the worlds of the living and the dead.

Now go on to the far end of this part of the gallery, to case 17 on the end wall.

The Yoruba god of iron is venerated by train drivers, pilots, barbers – anyone who uses metal things. With the slave trade, gods like these have spread to Brazil and Haiti. Masquerade has become carnival. You can also see a banner that shows the Fon gods of Benin, Nigeria. Their creator god is male and female, sun and moon.

Now return to the beginning of the gallery and go right to the other end to see more material from Benin.

The Oba (king) of Benin is believed to be a direct descendant of the legendary founder of the dynasty. Each year he performs rituals to honour his royal ancestors and to bring good fortune to his people. The mask was worn by the Oba, probably around his neck, during a ceremony to drive away evil. The pendant is decorated with the heads of the Portuguese who arrived in Benin in the 15th century.

Now return to the Ground floor and 24.

Brass plaque showing the Oba of Benin with attendants, Nigeria (16th century). (25) Plaques like this were fixed to pillars in the Oba's palace in Benin City.

Maya (200 BC–AD 1000)

Incas (1200–1534)   Aztecs (1325–1521)

Easter Island head (1400)

Central America: ritual and sacrifice, _Room 27_
From **24** go through **26**, North America, on the right to **27**, Mexico. Turn to your left to the red wall.

The Maya of ancient Central America were ruled by priest-kings. Their religion focused on the struggle to achieve a balance between the forces of fertility and life against those of drought, war and famine, enacted in the ritual ball game. Major Maya monuments show scenes of blood-letting as part of ritual preparations for royal accession. Yaxchilán Lintel 16 shows Lord Bird jaguar IV in warrior garb, standing over a captive whose nose and cheek bear drops of blood. The capture of sacrificial victims was an essential part of Maya warfare.

The later Aztecs in Mexico built on the religious heritage of the Maya. There was an enormous increase in human sacrifice, since the gods of a vast and complicated pantheon needed constant sacrifice in a universe seen as profoundly unstable.

In the long blue case find this knife (_see below_) at the back. An eagle warrior forms the handle of this knife used to cut the hearts out of sacrificial victims. Eagles and snakes, as sky and water beings in constant conflict, are common symbols in Mesoamerica. The Aztec capital Tenochtitlan was founded,

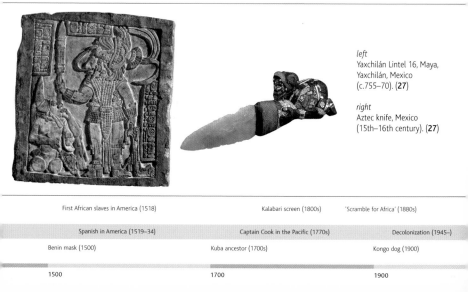

left
Yaxchilán Lintel 16, Maya, Yaxchilán, Mexico (c.755–70). (**27**)

right
Aztec knife, Mexico (15th–16th century). (**27**)

First African slaves in America (1518)

Kalabari screen (1800s)

'Scramble for Africa' (1880s)

Spanish in America (1519–34)

Captain Cook in the Pacific (1770s)

Decolonization (1945–)

Benin mask (1500)

Kuba ancestor (1700s)

Kongo dog (1900)

1500

1700

1900

according to myth, where an eagle was seen perched on a cactus, a national symbol of Mexico to this day.

Now turn towards the other entrance to the gallery.

The serpent played an important role in Aztec religion. This one is a blend of realistic and mythical creatures. Others include a large stone rattlesnake carved with striking realism, and a double-headed serpent decorated with turquoise mosaic and red shell. Later in this tour you will see how some of these ideas in Mexico fused with those of the Christian missionaries.

North America: the natural world

The relation of man and nature in traditional Native North American society is based on a respect for animals, their power and cunning. Animals such as beavers and eagles appear as crests on poles like the one you can see in the Great Court. It tells the story of the Raven, creator of all things, stealing fish from a village at the bottom of the sea. Such poles are misleadingly called 'totem' poles, though they have nothing to do with totems, guardian spirits of the Algonquians in the Northeast.

Stone figure of Xiuhcoatl, Aztec, Mexico (1325–1521). (**27**)

Maya (200 BC–AD 1000)

Incas (1200–1534)   Aztecs (1325–1521)

Easter Island head (1400)

*Now return via **27** to **26**, the J.P. Morgan Chase Gallery of North America.*

Native North American peoples live in environments as varied as desert, plain, forest and seacoast. On your immediate right you can see Katsina dolls from the Hopi people of the arid Southwest. These dolls represent benign spirits who live with the Hopi for half the year, bringing harmony, fertility and rain to ensure a good crop of corn.

Now move along this wallcase to see the war shirt and headdress of a Blackfoot leader from the Canadian Plains *(case 13 panel 8)*. These are decorated with the animals and birds that the Blackfoot hunted or that represented their gods: thunderbirds, bison heads, tadpoles, eagle feathers, grizzly bear claws, bison horns, ermine and weasel fur. An ancestor figure, Scarface, was said to have received a weasel-tail costume from the sun. Later Blackfoot leaders like Red Crow *(see case 13 panel 6)* from the 1880s had to cope not only with European colonists and the demise of the buffalo, but also the threat to their traditions. Although baptized a Roman Catholic, he retained his Native religion and fought the attempt to suppress the Blackfoot Sun Dance.

Shaman's mask, Yup'ik, Alaska. (**26**, *case 9 by door into* **24**). This mask is part human, part fox. Shamans look for the causes of illnesses in the soul as much as in the body, and seek to remove them. You can find out more about shamans in **24**, *case 9*.

First African slaves in America (1518)

Kalabari screen (1800s)   'Scramble for Africa' (1880s)

Spanish in America (1519–34)   Captain Cook in the Pacific (1770s)   Decolonization (1945–)

Benin mask (1500)   Kuba ancestor (1700s)   Kongo dog (1900)

1500   1700   1900

Hohao (spirit board), Elema people, Papua New Guinea (late 19th–early 20th century). (**24**, *case 1 nearest to the Great Court*)

*Now leave the gallery and turn left in **24** and go round to the other side of the case on North America.*

In central case 4 (facing the Easter Island head) is a painted wooden model of the same Haida pole you can see in the Great Court. The Eagle Beaver pole by the exit from **24** to the Great Court also comes from British Columbia and celebrates the encounter between ancestors and helpful animals.

Now find case 1, at the other side of the Easter Island head, and look for this spirit board.

The Pacific world

The figure on this carved and painted board depicts a forest spirit known to the coastal people of the Papuan Gulf. Spirits housed in a board like this one helped to bring success in hunting. Boards were kept inside a men's ceremonial house, and were occasionally repainted and presented with offerings in order to keep the spirits in a good humour.

Hawaiian open-air temples were dedicated to the three main Hawaiian deities, who represented war, life and prosperity. This large and intimidating figure of the god of war (*left*) was erected by a chief, seeking the god's support in war. The figure has a characteristic

right
Wooden temple image of a war god, Hawaii (1795–1819). *Not currently on display.*

open mouth, and in his hair are stylized pigs heads, possibly symbolic of the god and wealth. Temple worship was restricted to the chiefly classes in Hawaii, and was accompanied by elaborate ceremony and offerings, often of human sacrifice.

This dress (*below*) was worn by the chief mourner, either a priest or a close relative, of an important deceased person. He carried a menacing long club edged with shark teeth, and led a procession of mourners through the local area, attacking anyone not complying with mourning taboos.

Cultures today

Popular religions today combine traditions old and new with organized world religions. Here are examples from the Americas, Asia and Afghanistan.

The celebration of the festivals of All Saints and All Souls in Mexico is a joyful and ironic commemoration of the dead who, according to popular belief, come back for two days each November. In this fusion of Christianity and pre-Columbian ancestor beliefs, death is represented through sugar skulls, paper stencils and papier mâché figures. The Linares family of Mexico City specialize in large-

left
Mourner's dress, Society Islands, French Polynesia (18th century).
Not currently on display

right
Victor Jupurrula Ross, Yarla Jukurrpa ('Bush Potato Dreaming'), painting, Northern Territory, Australia (1987). © 2000 Victor Jupurrula Ross.

First African slaves in America (1518)	Kalabari screen (1800s)	'Scramble for Africa' (1880s)
Spanish in America (1519–34)	Captain Cook in the Pacific (1770s)	Decolonization (1945–)
Benin mask (1500)	Kuba ancestor (1700s)	Kongo dog (1900)
1500	1700	1900

scale figures like The Atomic Apocalypse, part of which is displayed here. It refers to the bombing of Hiroshima and Nagasaki in 1945, the Biafran War (1966–70) and Ayatollah Khomeini in Iran. These four horsemen bring war, famine, disease and death, one brandishing an atom bomb. For Dürer's image of the Horsemen of the Apocalypse see Tour 3 *(p.45)*.

below left
Day of the Dead figures, papier mâché, Linares Brothers, Mexico (1980s). **(24)**

below right
Gold pectoral, Calima, Colombia (100–1500). **(24)** Its shape suggests the eagle, symbol of the sun and of enormous power as it soars into the sky.

Now turn to the far corner of the gallery to see startling carnival costumes from Bolivia.

Masks like these are made for the Dance of the Devils that is part of the annual carnival celebration in the mining town of Oruro in the Bolivian Andes.

The devil in the mine embodied the life-giving but dangerous power of the earth.

At the back of this case are examples of offerings made by the Incas of Peru to their gods.

Now cross the gallery to the other freestanding case, for the Nicobar Islands.

As in other parts of the Indian Ocean, many people in the Nicobar Islands are now Christian or Muslim. However, they also maintain many traditional practices, including elaborate ceremonies carried out to avert or overcome misfortune. This board was used to enlist the help of fish, animals, and mermaids. If the ritual was successful the board was hung

Maya (200 BC–AD 1000)

Incas (1200–1534)   Aztecs (1325–1521)

Easter Island head (1400)

in the house to ensure future health. It was invoked every new moon in order to retain its healing effect or its power to ward off malevolent spirits.

Now go to the wallcase behind for other examples of warding off evil. Among the Turkmen nomads of Afghanistan, boys are protected from snakes, scorpions, disease, accidents and the 'evil eye', which threatens life itself. A whole range of items are attached to their clothes: bells, beads, amulets, coins, feathers, shells, tufts of hair, models of sharp tools and weapons, tubes containing texts or prayers from the Qur'an, and snakes modelled in cloth.

In Asia, replicas of motor-bikes, telephones, money and other symbols of worldly success are burnt by some Chinese communities as offerings to recently deceased relatives. They form part of an elaborate funeral ceremony, helping to ease the passage of the souls of the dead through limbo and purgatory.

This gallery contrasts Western lifestyles and attitudes to health and well-being with those in many other cultures. Religion and ritual play a big part in how these cultures explain and deal with illness and disaster. The central installation on the other hand shows a Western perspective in medical technology addressing the physical aspects of illness largely in isolation.

below left
Bolivian devil mask (1985). (**24**)

below right
Afghan boy's tunic (early 20th century). (**24**)

First African slaves in America (1518) Kalabari screen (1800s) 'Scramble for Africa' (1880s)

Spanish in America (1519–34) Captain Cook in the Pacific (1770s) Decolonization (1945–)

Benin mask (1500) Kuba ancestor (1700s) Kongo dog (1900)

1500 1700 1900

Further reading

General

Apostolos-Cappadona, Diane, *Dictionary of Women in Religious Art*. Oxford, 1998

Barley, Nigel, *Dancing on the Grave: Encounters with Death*. John Murray, 1995

Bowker, John, *God. A Brief History*. Dorling Kindersley, 2002

Coleman, Simon and Elsner, John, *Pilgrimage*. British Museum Press, 1995

Cooper, J. C., *An Illustrated Encyclopaedia of Traditional Symbols*. Thames & Hudson, 1978

Crumlin, Rosemary (ed.), *Beyond Belief: Modern Art and the Religious Imagination*. National Gallery of Victoria, 1998

Fernández-Armesto, Felipe (intro), *World of Myths: Volume Two*. British Museum Press, 2004

Onians, John (ed.), *Atlas of World Art*. Laurence King, 2004

Paine, Crispin (ed.), *Godly Things: Museums, Objects and Religion*. Cassell, 2000

Palmer, Martin (ed.), *The Times World Religions*. Times Books, 2002

Reeve, John (ed.), *Sacred*. British Library, 2007

Richards, Chris (ed.), *Illustrated Encylopedia of World Religions*. Element, 1997

Sheridan, Alison (ed.), *Heaven and Hell, and other worlds of the dead*. National Museums of Scotland, 2000

Smart, Ninian, *The World's Religions*. Cambridge, 2nd edn 1998

Warner, Marina (intro), *World of Myths: Volume One*. British Museum Press, 2005

Africa

Girshick Ben-Amos, Paula, *The Art of Benin*. British Museum Press, 2nd edn 1994

Mack, John (ed.), *Africa: Arts and Cultures*. British Museum Press, 2005

Americas

Carmichael, Elizabeth and Sayer, Chloe, *The Skeleton at the Feast: The Day of the Dead in Mexico*. British Museum Press, 1991

King, J.C.H., *First Peoples, First Contacts: Native Peoples of North America*. British Museum Press, 1999

McEwan, Colin, *Ancient Mexico in the British Museum*. British Museum Press, 1994

Ancient World

Black, Jeremy and Green, Anthony, *Gods, Demons and Symbols of Ancient Mesopotamia: An Illustrated Dictionary*. British Museum Press, revised edn 2004

Mitchell, Terence, *The Bible in the British Museum*. British Museum Press, 2007

Quirke, Stephen, *Ancient Egyptian Religion*. British Museum Press, 1992

Taylor, John, *Death and the Afterlife in Ancient Egypt*. British Museum Press, 2001

Buddhism

Bechert, H. and Gombrich, R., *The World of Buddhism*. Thames & Hudson, 1984

Fisher, Robert E., *Buddhist Art and Architecture*. Thames & Hudson, 1993

Knox, Robert, *Amaravati: Buddhist Sculpture from the Great Stupa*. British Museum Press, 1992

McArthur, Meher, *Reading Buddhist Art*. Thames & Hudson, 2002

Pemberton, Delia, *The Buddha*. British Museum Press, 2007

Portal, Jane, *Korea: Art and Archaeology*. British Museum Press, 2000

Zwalf, Wladimir, *Buddhism: Art and Faith*. British Museum Press, 1985

Zwalf, Wladimir, *Heritage of Tibet*. British Museum Press, 1981

China

Birrell, Anne, *Chinese Myths*. British Museum Press, 2000

Michaelson, Carol and Portal, Jane, *Chinese Art in Detail*. British Museum Press, 2006

Rawson, Jessica (ed.), *The British Museum Book of Chinese Art*. British Museum Press, revised edn 2007

Christianity

Carey, Frances (ed.), *The Apocalypse and the Shape of Things to Come*. British Museum Press, 1999

Cormack, Robin, *Icons*. British Museum Press, 2007

Harries, Richard and Mayr-Harting, Henry (eds), *Christianity: 2,000 Years*. Oxford, 2002

Loverance, Rowena, *Christ*. British Museum Press, 2004

Loverance, Rowena, *Christian Art*. British Museum Press, 2007

MacGregor, Neil, *Seeing Salvation: Images of Christ in Art*. Yale/National Gallery, 2000

Murray, Peter and Linda, *Oxford Companion to Christian Art and Architecture*. Oxford, 1998

Hinduism

Blurton, T. Richard, *Bengali Myths*. British Museum Press, 2007

Blurton, T. Richard, *Hindu Art*. British Museum Press, 2002

Dallapiccola, A.L., *Hindu Myths*. British Museum Press, 2003

Dallapiccola, A.L., *Hindu Visions of the Sacred*. British Museum Press, 2004

Dallapiccola, A.L., *Indian Art in Detail*. British Museum Press, 2007

Knott, Kim, *Hinduism: A Very Short Introduction*. Oxford, 2000

Islam

Brend, Barbara, *Islamic Art*. British Museum Press, 1991, reprint 2005

Canby, Sheila, *Islamic Art in Detail*. British Museum Press, 2006

Porter, Venetia, *Word into Art: Artists of the Modern Middle East*. British Museum Press, 2006

Ruthven, Malise, *Islam: A Very Short Introduction*. Oxford, 1997

Jainism

Cort, John, *Jains in the World: Religious Values and Ideology in India*. Oxford, 2001

Pal, Pratapaditya (ed.), *Peaceful Liberators: Jain Art from India*. Thames & Hudson, 1994

Judaism

Jacobs, Louis, *The Jewish Religion: A Companion*. Oxford, 1995

Kedourie, Elie (ed.), *The Jewish World*. Thames & Hudson, 1979

Solomon, Norman, *Judaism: A Very Short Introduction*. Oxford, 2000

Pacific cultures

Hooper, Steven, *Pacific Encounters: Art and Divinity in Polynesia 1760–1860*. British Museum Press, 2006

Starzecka, D.C. (ed.), *Maori: Art and Culture*. British Museum Press, 2nd edn 1998

Van Tilburg, Jo Anne, *Easter Island*. British Museum Press, 1994

Shintō

Harris, Victor (ed.), *Shintō: The Sacred Art of Ancient Japan*. British Museum Press, 2001

Sikhism

Nesbitt, Eleanor, *Sikhism: A Very Short Introduction*. Oxford, 2005

Serpent demon, dancer's mask, Sri Lanka (19th century). (**24**)

Other Museums

Britain and Ireland
Bath, Museum of East Asian Art:
www.meaaa.org.uk
Cambridge, Fitzwilliam Museum:
www.fitzmuseum.cam.ac.uk
Dublin, Chester Beatty Library and
National Museum:
www.cbl.ie
www.museum.ie
Durham:
Oriental.Museum@durham.ac.uk
Edinburgh:
www.nms.ac.uk
Glasgow, St Mungo Museum of Religious
Life and Art:
www.glasgowmuseums.com
London, Horniman Museum:
www.horniman.ac.uk
London, Jewish Museum:
www.jewishmuseum.org.uk
London, The Victoria and Albert Museum:
www.vam.ac.uk
Manchester, Jewish Museum:
www.manchesterjewishmuseum.com
Oxford, Ashmolean and Pitt-Rivers Museums:
www.ashmol.ox.ac.uk
www.prm.ox.ac.uk/japan

Europe
Belgium
Musées Royaux d'Art et d'Histoire, Brussels:
www.kmkg-mrah.be
France
Louvre, Paris:
www.louvre.fr
Musée Guimet, Paris:
www.museeguimet.fr
Germany
Museum für Ostasiatische Kunst:
www.smb.spk-berlin.de
Netherlands
Rijksmuseum, Amsterdam:
www.rijksmuseum.nl
National Museum of Ethnology, Leiden:
www.rmv.nl
Museum Het Catharijneconvent, Utrecht:
www.catherijneconvent.nl
Sweden
World Culture Museum, Gothenburg:
www.varldskulturmuseet.se
Switzerland
Museum Rietberg: www.rietberg.ch

USA
www.artcyclopedia.com
Art Institute of Chicago:
www.artic.edu
Asian Art Museum, San Francisco:
www.asianart.org; www.search.famsf.org
Asia Society of New York:
www.asiasociety.org
Cleveland Museum of Art:
www.clevelandart.org
Honolulu Academy of Arts:
www.honoluluacademy.org
Library of Congress:
www.loc.gov/exhibits/ukiyo-e/japan
Los Angeles County Museum of Art:
www.lacma.org
Metropolitan Museum, New York:
www.metmuseum.org
Museum of Fine Arts, Boston:
www.mfa.org
Nelson-Atkins Museum, Kansas City:
www.nelson-atkins.org
New York Public Library:
www.nypl.org
Peabody-Essex Museum, Salem:
www.pem.org
Philadelphia Museum of Art:
www.philamuseum.org
Sackler Freer Gallery, Washington DC:
www.asia.si.edu
St Louis University, Museum of Contemporary
Religious Art:
www.slu.edu

Index

Upper floors

Rooms
35
41
45–59
61–66
68–73
90–94

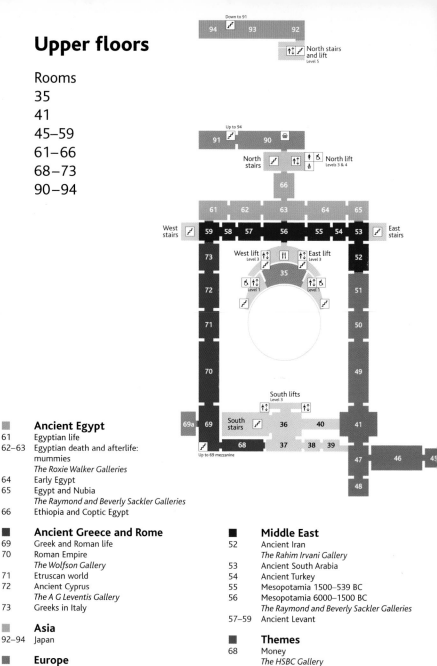

Ancient Egypt
61   Egyptian life
62–63   Egyptian death and afterlife:
     mummies
     The Roxie Walker Galleries
64   Early Egypt
65   Egypt and Nubia
     The Raymond and Beverly Sackler Galleries
66   Ethiopia and Coptic Egypt

Ancient Greece and Rome
69   Greek and Roman life
70   Roman Empire
     The Wolfson Gallery
71   Etruscan world
72   Ancient Cyprus
     The A G Leventis Gallery
73   Greeks in Italy

Asia
92–94   Japan

Europe
41   Europe 300–1100
45   The Waddesdon Bequest
46   Europe 1400–1800
47   Europe 1800–1900
48   Europe 1900 to the present
49   Roman Britain
     The Weston Gallery
50   Britain and Europe 800 BC–AD 43
51   Europe and the Middle East 10,000–800 BC

Middle East
52   Ancient Iran
     The Rahim Irvani Gallery
53   Ancient South Arabia
54   Ancient Turkey
55   Mesopotamia 1500–539 BC
56   Mesopotamia 6000–1500 BC
     The Raymond and Beverly Sackler Galleries
57–59   Ancient Levant

Themes
68   Money
     The HSBC Gallery

Exhibitions and changing displays
35   Special exhibitions
     The Joseph Hotung Great Court Gallery
69a   Changing displays
90   Prints and drawings
91   Asia